MAKING SCHOOLS AND FAMILIES SUCCESSFUL

MAKING SCHOOLS AND FAMILIES SUCCESSFUL

How to Unify Students, Parents, and Teachers

Joseph W. Gauld

ROWMAN & LITTLEFIELD
Lanham • Boulder • New York • London

Published by Rowman & Littlefield
An imprint of The Rowman & Littlefield Publishing Group, Inc.
4501 Forbes Boulevard, Suite 200, Lanham, Maryland 20706
www.rowman.com

6 Tinworth Street, London SE11 5AL

British Library Cataloguing in Publication Information Available

Library of Congress Cataloging-in-Publication Data Available

Names: Gauld, Joseph W., author.
Title: Making schools and families successful : how to unify students, parents, and teachers
/ Joseph W. Gauld.
Description: Lanham : Rowman & Littlefield, [2021] | Includes index. | Summary: "Schools
will learn to first emphasize cooperation and unity, which would create a successful
school culture; one encouraging competition with respect rather than arrogance"—
Provided by publisher.
Identifiers: LCCN 2021010684 (print) | LCCN 2021010685 (ebook) | ISBN
9781475859485 (cloth) | ISBN 9781475859492 (ebook)
Subjects: LCSH: Home and school. | Education—Parent participation.
Classification: LCC LC225 .G38 2021 (print) | LCC LC225 (ebook) | DDC 371.19/2—dc23
LC record available at https://lccn.loc.gov/2021010684
LC ebook record available at https://lccn.loc.gov/2021010685

I dedicate this book to my parents; my wife, children, and grandchildren; my colleagues, students, and their parents; and others who helped inspire the wisdom in me that I hope will contribute to yours.

CONTENTS

Foreword   ix

Prologue   xi

Preface   xv

Introduction   xvii

PART I: THE FOUNDATION OF THE UNIFYING PROCESS OF GROWTH   **I**

I Unique Potential: The Essential Ingredient   3

2 Character: The Unique Potential Creator   11

3 The Unifying Five Principles: Guiding the Process   25

4 The Unifying Culture: Roles and Responsibilities   41

PART II: TOOLS: HOW TO PRACTICE THE UNIFYING PROCESS   **77**

5 Head, Heart, Soul: The Hierarchy in Unifying Learning 79

6 The Action-Reflection Learning Cycle   109

7 Rigor, Synergy, Conscience: Progressive Levels of
    Learning   129

8 Unifying Academics: Pathway to Excellence   147

PART III: ADVANCING THE UNIFYING PROCESS TO EXCELLENCE   **171**

9 The Unifying Family Learning Center   173

10 The Unifying Inner Leadership Model: Five Deliverables   199

Index   217
About the Author   225

FOREWORD

Dear Reader,

First, full disclosure: I am a parent whose family was transformed by the educational process described in this book. Our family started at the Hyde School in Maine in 1987; at our first interview, Joe Gauld looked at my husband and me and said, "What you don't understand is that you people have the problem!" It didn't take long to understand what, so baffling at the time, was true: we talked about character (don't lie, don't cheat), but we lived in an achievement culture that put emphasis on where we vacationed, what neighborhood we lived in, what kind of car we drove, how much money we made. Our "character speeches" were drowned out.

It did not take long for me to see that the Unifying kind of education described in these pages—where teachers were concerned not only about my child's academics but even more about his character, as well as their own, and where parents were asked to become role models of character and put principles at the center of their homes—was the kind of education that all children and families deserved. Regardless of color, race, or creed, this kind of education needed to be spread across America.

What I loved most about the Unifying program was the partnership we had with the school: the trust I had in the faculty allowed me to let them hold my child accountable when needed; again, character was what mattered most. Thus, I was thrilled when, in 1993, I was asked to head the Family Education Department at one of Hyde's early public school partnerships, the Hyde Leadership School in New Haven, Connecticut. I was given a chance to pass on this framework!

This public magnet school brought teachers, parents, and students together in the Unifying program, which helped transform families in an inner-city community. At graduation, students made the same kind of speeches to their families and teachers you will read in this book. But most important, the kids had visions for their lives and they knew themselves and what it would take to fulfill their dreams.

This educational process works. I've seen it in the Pennsylvania schools that Joe refers to; I've been a part of it in the Hyde Schools in New York City; I've seen it work in communities that have adopted it for their organization or workplace.

If you are an educator, involved in education, or just interested in developing strong, healthy, self-aware, and motivated kids, read what Joe teaches in this book. If you are a parent and want a deeper relationship with your kids, read this book. And please don't wait. All kids deserve this kind of education.

                                                    Pam Hardy

PROLOGUE

This book came out of my 1962 commitment to find a better way to prepare kids for life. Now, more than a half century later, I feel confident in the schools, administrators, teachers, parents, and students who are developing that better way.

Students and Teachers Singing School Song to Parents. *Hyde School*

Meanwhile, the educational system I sought to change has remained an undaunted fortress, in spite of its ever-increasing problems. Why?

Some might say people just resist change—a lot of truth in that. But I think more has to do with parental attitudes.

As tailenders of the Greatest Generation, our parents emphasized character and were very much in control. However, after World War II, the GI Bill gave us free schooling, and schools soon became important in preparing students for the best colleges.

Thus, parents ceded a lot of their authority to the school (message to their kids: "Get good grades"). Once parents ceded this top position to the school, they couldn't also turn around and then demand character growth, so they slipped back to a less demanding role, one that persists today: child protector. Comparing this parental attitude with that of parents of the Greatest Generation would be amusing.

I think a by-product of this attitude is parents seeking a relationship or "love" from their children. This undermines the deeper relationship parents should have in being dedicated to preparing children for life by helping them realize their best and become self-sufficient by age nineteen.

This weaker parent leadership has contributed to a stronger youth culture, which in turn has been greatly strengthened by the Internet. It is not a healthy situation.

Whatever the authority of parents and schools, the youth culture allows adolescents latitude in their actions, morals, and behaviors that can encourage their worst. But they generally do not realize that once they enter the adult world, except for a small group, the youth culture is gone, and they are accountable for everything they do. The pressure of this is such that some don't recover, while a number of others get stuck and never find the opportunity to explore their unique potential.

I believe this is why you see a number of twentysomethings struggling today.

Now that I've got that off my chest, let me say I have great enthusiasm for what our nation can accomplish, and I believe we can build an educational system that will inspire the world and help us build a democracy beyond anything we have imagined.

PREFACE

So what are my hopes for this book?

- I hope it contributes to helping solidly restore parents, family, and the home as the primary influence and basic foundation of child-rearing, while helping empower parents to assume that leadership.
- I hope it helps teachers develop a better partnership with their students, and begin to open a dialogue with their students' parents.
- I hope school administrators will give some of these ideas a try, particularly our Discovery Group homeroom plan that has worked so well in some Pennsylvania public schools.
- I hope others, curious about the process, will become supporters.

Then there is an expectation I have.

Ever since Russia launched Sputnik in 1957, there have been continual efforts, without success, to reform American education. In our capitalistic system, it would have been replaced long ago, but education is a government-run monopoly, plus change is difficult to accept. So the failures of this obsolete and unsound system just grow. Cheating and bullying are now normal. Who would have thought fifty years ago that schools would become no longer safe, that school shootings would become a regular occurrence?

The purpose of today's system is to develop academic proficiency. Yet only roughly one-third of American students meet that standard on tests.

This obsolete/unsound system is giving our society a great deal of pain. Clearly it breeds inequality. How much more will it take before we demand change?

When that time comes, hopefully, some exciting new concept will be proving itself, and a critical mass of Americans will be ready to give it a try. And we'll be off and running.

In the meantime, we offer the Hyde process, a better way to educate children and support families.

INTRODUCTION

I deeply believe in the principles that founded this great country, that revere equality and individuality, making us all deserving of dignity and worth. So it pains me to say I believe that over the last seventy years, schools and families have increasingly failed to help American children grow and develop their potentials. Today's educational system primarily values the academic proficiency of children, one small measure of their overall capabilities. I think the vast majority of schools and parents don't understand kids well enough to realize how this system impedes the natural growth of children.

Visit any kindergarten class in America and you will note incoming children so eager to learn, they raise their hands to answer questions to which they don't even know the answer. A 2015 Gallup poll found that 75 percent of fifth-graders "engaged" in learning, and that number keeps dropping to 32 percent for eleventh-graders—without counting school dropouts.[1]

Consider what today's educational system accomplishes with those children:

- Bullying and cheating are rampant. These behaviors demean children, but it's how they cope with the unnatural competitive environment thrust upon them.
- School shootings are commonplace. Adults have blindly made an "in-house" problem worse by applying an "outside" solution—guns, drills, guards—thus transforming what was once a sanctuary into something children now feel is unsafe. The real solution will come from "inside": a new family-school bond.
- Our schools have helped establish an academic cultural pecking order: Asian, White, Black, Hispanic. In 2016 the US Department of Education reported these percentages of college-age Americans holding bachelor's degrees: Asian, 53.9; White, 38.2; Black, 22.5; Hispanic, 15.5.[2]
- Family wealth powerfully influences SATs and educational opportunities. A Georgetown University study entitled "Born to Win, Schooled to Lose" found that the odds of working at a good entry-level job at age twenty-five were 70 percent for a child who came from an affluent family but had a low math score in kindergarten, and only 31 percent for a child who came from an economically disadvantaged family but had a high math score in kindergarten.[3]

Our educational system is controlled by the wealthy; further, compared with other nations, our system produces essentially mediocre academic proficiency scores. There is a deeper problem with our education system: unlike our democracy, it had no founding philosophy, and thus no basic purpose and principles to guide its development.

With family and community centering society, our founding fathers saw education in broad terms of character development involving the entire community; "school" was a place for a primary focus on literacy and knowledge. So lacking a philosophical structure, our educational system has been formed politically, with decisions often made by a privileged few.

Our educational behavior has become ridiculous. Education for children is a far deeper process than college or job prep. Socrates defined the goal of education as "Know thyself," and Plato said, "The unexamined life is not worth living."

Education should first and foremost be designed to help children develop. An overwhelming academic focus does not fit their natural growth. They first need a primary focus on their emotional and social growth; they don't even start thinking logically and abstractly until age eleven.[4]

As an adult, I was a part of this system beginning in 1951. I loved teaching, coaching, and administrating, and I was committed to the lives of my students. But I experienced a crisis of conscience on New Year's Eve in 1962 when I realized what we were doing was not reaching the deeper potentials of kids—and there had to be a better way to prepare them for life.

This book describes the better way I found that ended up involving both schools and families.

What makes schools and families "good," or even highly successful? They, like all organizations, are made up of a group of people. So the larger question might be: What makes groups highly successful? Daniel Coyle provides a vital clue in his groundbreaking book *Culture Code: The Secrets of Highly Successful Groups.*

Coyle studied highly successful groups and organizations and found that their key "secret" was making all members feel they really belonged, which meant creating a culture where they felt safe enough to be vulnerable. Once this was achieved, members became deeply unified and powerfully productive.

Consider this example Coyle gives: Different groups were given twenty strands of uncooked spaghetti, a yard each of transparent tape and string to build the tallest structure possible, plus a marshmallow to put on top. Here is how some groups accomplished the task, measured in the height of their structures:

- Business students: 10 inches
- Lawyers: 15 inches
- CEOs: 22 inches
- Kindergartners: 28 inches

The superiority of the kindergartners was attributed to their ability to focus on the problem, whereas the others were held back by observing adult protocols and avoiding vulnerability. The kindergartners worked as a team with one mind. Feeling safe and therefore vulnerable, the five-year-olds proved that truly working together creates a powerful synergy.

If we apply this wisdom to our standard educational system, we immediately see the system's mediocrity. Bullying and cliques in schools are such that some students are afraid to go to school. Students are put in competition with each other rather than taught how to work together and respect each other.

Nor do schools actively seek a cooperative working relationship with students or with their parents and families, the latter being by far the largest influence in a student's life.

After seventy years of teaching—including forty-five years of in-depth work with parents and families—I am convinced this system ignores the natural growth of children and is often in conflict with it. Studies have shown that students today generally lack motivation and involvement in their studies, instead engaging in widespread cheating, bullying, self-doubt, and other problems.

In developing public speaking confidence in students, something I have been doing for some years at the Hyde School in Maine, I constantly have to address students' passivity and their fear of speaking aloud with their own voice. However receptive this passivity might make them to traditional academic teaching, it tends to shut down their exploration of their own unique potential.

The great aim of education is not knowledge but action.
—Herbert Spencer

As adults in life, we realize we must replace passivity with a self-assuring—even commanding—voice. Students do have that voice, especially on the playground (*HEY! THROW ME THE BALL!*), so I help them transform their school voice into their playground voice.

Basically, our present educational system doesn't seek to help the individual student; it focuses on improving test scores, college admissions, and job statistics.

This system can't handle the rebel—someone close to America's heart. The system loves what I call the "smiling zero," someone who simply doesn't make any waves in school. But it goes to war against the student who rebels against or challenges the status quo.

Of course some rebels just feel a sense of entitlement. But I more often see a great independent spirit in rebels; they challenge the system to see if the people behind it are worth trusting with their lives. Many ultimately become leaders themselves.

Trouble is only opportunity in work clothes.—Henry J. Kaiser

Those "smiling zeros" have a unique potential, like all kids, and need to be challenged to discover their strengths, weaknesses, and long-term potential. Kids naturally grow far more from active than passive or intellectual pursuits, yet schools offer active learning opportunities primarily only as "extracurriculars." Talented or motivated students seek them; the rest become spectators or simply miss out.

It's an embarrassing reality that today's educational system sees little difference in the responsibilities of twelfth-graders compared to first-graders. For example, both need a note from adults to excuse lateness, underlining that all students are treated as children. Instead, schools need to focus on active learning, as well as emotional and social growth, emphasizing character development. As proven with more than fifty years of Hyde School graduates, Hyde's Unifying process of education inspires student motivation and a sense of purpose, while it empowers self-confidence.

Hyde charter schools demonstrate that this new educational process works in public schools as well as independent schools. We have two charters in New York City. Hyde Leadership Public Charter School in the Bronx has more than one thousand students. Located in one of the country's poorest districts, where only 49 percent of students even graduate from high school, Hyde Leadership excels: more than 90 percent of the first graduating class went to college, from which nearly 50 percent graduated, five times the rate for similar disadvantaged districts. Now with eight graduating classes, over 70 percent of the graduates are in college or have graduated.

We have helped a cluster of Pennsylvania school systems become dedicated to developing the unique potential and character of each student. Their school cultures establish and nurture Discovery Groups, which include students of mixed grades with a teacher; the groups meet regularly to do group activities and to share their lives.

In Discovery Groups, more action—intramurals, performing arts, community service, jobs—is introduced into the curriculum; each Discovery Group sits together at an appointed time to share and reflect on their experiences. It serves as their Unifying process. Eventually, parents become an important part of these groups and the school community.

Statistics: after just four months in our newest public school using our Discovery Group process, 95 percent of both students and teachers liked and wanted to keep this program; 89 percent of parents supported it.

In Hyde's oldest public school, in Halifax, Pennsylvania, discipline problems decreased 91 percent over a ten-year period. In the first five years of Pennsylvania state testing, English and mathematics proficiency scores rose from 72 to 80 percent and 69 to 80 percent, respectively, with fewer failures.[5]

Building a powerful school culture of trust and motivation prepares young people for meaningful and fulfilling lives, with college and jobs an integral part of that preparation.

But there is a major roadblock we must tackle before we will be able to build this dynamic school culture more pervasively. The barrier is an educational system built on the premise that students are passive recipients of learning rather than active practitioners individually responsible for their learning.

With no defined philosophy, the system's de facto philosophy is simply achieving the academic proficiency of the student. While it may satisfy adult purposes, it only superficially addresses the heavily emotional and social aspects of a student's growth.

While education sometimes recognizes this, its reform efforts—character education, social and emotional learning, and personalized learning—have generally been limited in effectiveness, because the main focus remains on the intellect, and the tail cannot wag the dog.

More recently, the app TikTok[6] has made its way into many classrooms because it serves to motivate students. But since the educational system has no formal philosophy and principles to guide it, this will likely be another short-lived fad.

Horace Mann, the father of American public schools, said given a year to teach spelling, he'd spend the first nine months on motivation. This respect for the student's role is fundamental in the Unifying process.

A Unified School Community has been proven to accomplish these educational goals:

- Reach the deepest motivation in students
- Bond teachers, parents, and students into a powerful team
- Elevate teachers to guide the entire growth process of youngsters
- Strengthen the family and empower parents as primary teachers

This book is designed to help create fully functioning Unified School Communities and families. While primarily directed to administrators and teachers, it can also help parents and students understand their new roles in the education process. It serves to unify the efforts of all community members.

It can also serve parents who seek to develop fully functioning families.

TRADITIONAL EDUCATION VS. UNIFIED EDUCATION

The Unifying process focuses on the individual student's unique potential and thus transforms the entire learning process, creating new roles for the subject, student, and teacher alike. If we imagine teacher, subject, and student as three vertices of a learning triangle, then the base of the traditional triangle is teacher-subject, which then determines the third vertex: the student. However, the base of the Unified triangle is teacher-student, which then determines the third vertex: the subject.

In short, the essential Unified partnership becomes teacher-student, instead of the traditional teacher-subject. These fundamental changes then occur:

- The educational focus shifts from the subject to the student. The traditional subject is primarily learned in order to graduate, get into college, or get a job. The Unified subject is primarily learned as a vehicle to develop the unique potential and motivation of the student.
- The teacher becomes more of a coach than a professor. The traditional teacher tries to draw the student into the subject. The Unifying teacher tries to draw the subject into the personal development of the student.
- The student becomes more of an initiator than a follower. The traditional student simply has to meet or follow set standards of achievement. Regardless of achievement, the Unified student must continually demonstrate best effort and attitude in all aspects of school life.

This comparison sees traditional education as a rigid structure, controlled primarily by the subject and the teacher's interpretation or understanding of it. The Unified focus can be seen as being very fluid, with the teacher continually trying to connect the subject (and school life) to the unique potential of the student.

We see this approach as a win-win for both college preparation and student growth. The focus on the student inspires motivation, the biggest roadblock to present academic achievement.

Teacher Unifying with a Student. *Hyde School*

For a parent, here is the change in the learning triangle that applies to you: instead of primarily focusing on being an adult who knows what is best for your child's future, become the mentor who primarily shares his or her life experience with your child. This not only will give your child confidence, because he or she will begin to identify with you, but you will begin to develop a strong bond of trust. Deep sharing may seem very difficult at first, but the results will show it is well worth it.

Unified teaching not only builds on the deeper self-discovery motivation in students, but also better fits their varied talents and learning styles. And it draws out the deeper personal skills within the teacher. The Myers-Briggs personality test indicates that nearly 90 percent of us are a great deal more comfortable dealing with people or action than with academic abstractions.[7] Indeed, Dr. Howard Gardner of Harvard University has identified eight distinct human intelligences, only two of which directly foster traditional academic achievement.[8]

Unifying teachers become adept at learning how to draw upon both the unique talents and the unique learning styles of students, which ultimately will maximize both the students' growth *and* their academic achievement.

This is why we say, *Put character first, and the academics will follow.* For those concerned this focus might undercut traditional academic performance, recall that in the first public school to adopt the Hyde process, student scores on state English and math tests increased significantly over the first five years.

THE NEED TO "REPROGRAM" OURSELVES

Very few of us are ready to tackle the task of developing unique potential in youngsters, because our own education pointed us in a different direction. Few of us were helped to understand who we are and what our lives could be. Our own educational experience taught us to look *outside* ourselves to gain knowledge, not to search *inside* in order to "know thyself," as the ancient Greeks would have taught us to do.

It is a miracle that curiosity survives formal education.
—Albert Einstein

The search for unique potential begins with three fundamental questions:

- Who am I?
- Where am I going with my life?
- What do I need to get there?

But how could we learn to deal with these crucial life issues when our own progress in school was measured by how well we academically stacked up compared to others? We were deemed "successful" by simply getting honor grades, regardless of our effort, attitude, or character. We were never taught to value our growth above our achievements. Yes, we should be strongly motivated to achieve, but our desire for growth must be even stronger, or else we won't risk the mistakes and failures inherent in the challenges that draw out our best.

Very few of us were "programmed" to seek our unique potential. It is as if schools trained us as right-handers, and now we must learn how to become left-handers! So a major challenge to Hyde teachers and administrators (and parents) is to "reprogram" ourselves, to constantly examine this "right-handed" knowledge and achievement emphasis and then learn how to consistently both model and teach this new "left-handed" Unifying emphasis on self-discovery.

Thus, we need to have patience with establishing the United process not just in our schools, but also in our homes with development of our own unique potential and character. Sharing our personal struggles with our adolescents will be a major step in gaining their trust.

Of course, it must be mentioned that all students come from families, so a school's success in developing the concepts of challenge, respect, and excellence rests first and foremost on the efforts of parents in the home. The school's work in helping parents achieve this is of great benefit to family and school, and to their partnership.

So, in these pages, readers dedicated to improving their schools and families will find the philosophy, principles, mindset, experiences, practices, and methods that create a process able to reach the deeper potentials and spirit of students, as well as teachers and parents.

This process will also serve parents who are dedicated to seeking the best for their families.

NOTES

1. Ross Brenneman, "Gallup Student Poll Finds Engagement in School Dropping by Grade Level," *EducationWeek*, March 22, 2016, https://www.edweek.org/leadership/gallup-student-poll-finds-engagement-in-school-dropping-by-grade-level/2016/03.

2. Camille Ryan and Kurt Bauman, "Educational Attainment in the United States: 2015," US Census Bureau, US Department of Commerce, March 2016, https://www.census.gov/content/dam/Census/library/publications/2016/demo/p20-578.pdf.

3. Anthony Carnevale, Megan Fasules, Michael Quinn, Kathryn Campbell, "Born to Win, Schooled to Lose, Center on Education and the Workforce," Georgetown University, 2019, https://cew.georgetown.edu/cew-reports/schooled2lose.

4. "Abstract Thinking," PsychPedia, GoodTherapy, July 30, 2019, https://www.goodtherapy.org/blog/psychpedia/abstract-thinking.

5. Kristen A. Graham, "Philly Schools' Test Scores Mostly Rising, but Just 36% of Children Meet State English Standards," *Philadelphia Inquirer*, October 23, 2019, https://www.inquirer.com/education/philadelphia-schools-test-scores-reading-math-pssa-20191023.html.

6. Rachel Roderick, "How Teachers and Students Are Using TikTok in the Classroom," K12 Learning Liftoff, February 11, 2020, https://www.learningliftoff.com/tiktok-in-the-classroom.

7. Myers and Briggs Foundation, "The 16 MBTI Types," https://www.myersbriggs.org/my-mbti-personality-type/mbti-basics/the-16-mbti-types.htm.

8.   Kendra Cherry, "Gardner's Theory of Multiple Intelligences," Verywell Mind, July 17, 2019, https://www.verywellmind.com/gardners-theory-of-multiple-intelligences-2795161.

Part I

The Foundation of the Unifying Process of Growth

I

UNIQUE POTENTIAL

The Essential Ingredient

The entire Unifying process is built on this single premise: each of us is gifted with a unique potential that defines a destiny.

Every Unifying subject, activity, and teaching practice should first try to satisfy these questions: Will this help draw out or develop the unique potential of this student? Will this contribute to the overall development of unique potential?

The school community becomes unified by the personal development of students. Our goal is to graduate students who have a strong belief in their own sense of destiny, plus a genuine enthusiasm and proven competency to pursue it.

I would say so far Hyde has taught me how to be 100 percent myself. —Hyde student

A person's unique potential is like an "inner calling" and reflects his or her temperament, gifts, natural talents, passions, dreams, aspirations, backgrounds, and traditions. It is the person waiting to be born in each of us because of our own unique amalgamation of potentials and experience. It is what the ancient Greeks called one's *daimon:* a sort of perfect inner self that unfolds as we strive to fulfill our destinies.

It is not in the stars to hold our destiny but in ourselves.
—William Shakespeare

All of us grow up wanting to believe we have the potential to fulfill a higher purpose in life. Further, the concept of unique potential expresses the fundamental American belief that we all have dignity and worth. But pursuing this ideal for our lives isn't easy—and wasn't meant to be easy. We face an intense and lifelong challenge. We have difficulty holding on to this larger belief in ourselves. We find ourselves envying the talents of some. We see the obvious advantages—wealth, status, attractiveness, and so on—of others. We are nagged by our own disadvantages or shortcomings. In the end I suspect that most of us fulfill only a fraction of our deeper capabilities and the contributions we could make to the world.

What each must seek in his life never was on land or sea. It is something out of his own unique potentiality for experience, something that never has been and never could be experienced by anyone else.
—Joseph Campbell

Ralph Waldo Emerson was perhaps our greatest philosopher. He gave more than fifteen hundred speeches. Henry Thoreau was his protégé, with many outstanding Americans—like Walt Whitman and William James—following; Harvard named a building after Emerson.

The essence of Emerson's famous article on self-reliance is "a commitment to making decisions based on one's own native instinct, personal values, and primary experience over external advice, cultural conformity, and secondhand information." He believed in an individual's potential so strongly, it determined his educational philosophy: "The great object of education is to acquaint the youthful man with himself, to inspire in him self-trust."

Clearly, Emerson deeply believed that America's founding principles of individuality and equality must precede traditional educational efforts; a focus on developing youthful potentials must precede formal education.

A study to reaffirm this statement might consider: Thomas Edison did poorly and dropped out of elementary school. The Wright brothers were high school dropouts. Albert Einstein flunked algebra. Winston Churchill flunked his college entrance exam twice. Bill Gates and Steve Jobs were college dropouts.

Clearly, these exceptional individuals were inwardly focused on something much deeper than their formal education.

Most Americans believe everyone is born with that "special something," and the challenge is indicated in some of Emerson's quotes:

- "Insist on yourself; never imitate."
- "What lies behind you and what lies in front of you, pale in comparison to what lies inside of you."
- "Common sense is genius dressed in its working clothes."
- "Enthusiasm is the mother of effort, and without it nothing great was ever achieved."
- "Do the thing we fear, and death of fear is certain."

Emerson intensely encouraged youthful self-awareness and self-improvement; traditional education seeks youthful competition, always comparing oneself to others, which undermines Emerson's inner focus. No matter how well a youth may compete, there is always a "faster gun in the West."

Hyde believes that childhood holds the key to our true destinies, so while growing up we all need committed adults to help us prepare ourselves to pursue this larger dream. Together with parents/guardians, a dedicated Unified School Community can help us believe we have been uniquely gifted, as well as help us develop the strength of character needed as we experience life's challenges.

Is unique potential/destiny the end we seek, or is it the experiences that lead us to our vision? Is it a goal or a path? I suspect that both goal and path become a natural part of the deeper fulfillment we experience as we simply learn to do our best. People have found it helpful when I have answered this goal-path question thus: "If you are too goal oriented, think of your unique potential and destiny as a process; if you are too process oriented, think of unique potential as a goal." In other words, don't allow your own doubts, misperceptions, or impatience to get in the way; simply learn to do your best and trust nature to take care of the rest.

Fulfilling this unique potential/destiny process requires a strong and unwavering faith on our parts. It gives us little control over who we are, or what we are supposed to do with our lives. I personally felt cursed when I discovered my own gifts were centered in teaching, and once I graduated from college, I tried to run away from what I feared was my own unique potential. How could I ever become rich and famous if I were stuck in a classroom somewhere? Thank God my conscience has always been able to outvote my ego, because teaching has offered me a sense of worth and fulfillment I know I would never have found elsewhere.

If we did all the things we are capable of, we would literally astound ourselves. —Thomas Edison

How do we know we are on the right track to expressing our unique potential on the way to fulfilling our destiny? We don't, but we have the right guides: Always bet on the truth and doing the right thing by listening to conscience. Add patience, and I say you will end up with a life you feel is both meaningful and fulfilling.

Every man has his own destiny; the only imperative is to follow it, to accept it, no matter where it leads him. —Henry Miller

I say patience because I liken the pursuit of our destiny to that of a sailboat that has to make a series of tacks to reach its destination. At no time is it precisely headed to its destination, but it is always getting closer. I think the same is true for our serious pursuit of destiny.

A Hyde faculty must create a school environment that inspires this strong and unwavering faith in students, and thus leads them to ultimately be led by their own conscience. A Hyde School Community seems to be characterized by challenge, respect, and excellence:

- Challenge: Excitement in the form of challenge, curiosity, and exploration moves the school, which is balanced by the toughness of hard work and perseverance. Students, teachers, and parents who exemplify this searching dedication emerge as leaders. The school reflects a dynamic energy and

pioneer spirit, with complacency viewed as the ultimate enemy of growth.

- Respect: Since everyone is endowed with unique potential, a
  deep respect for all people emerges. Favoritism, cliques, or
  elitism are never tolerated in any form. It is a Hyde ethic to
  establish meaningful relationships with all others—an ethic
  that is particularly modeled by the faculty. The school generates a strong, even affectionate community bond.

- Excellence: A continual striving to fulfill one's best charac-
  terizes the school. We revere *unique potential* and insist that
  each person honor it with his or her best effort. In essence,
  each of us becomes a watchdog for and an integral part of
  the other's unique potential and destiny. *Brother's/Sister's
  Keeper* defines a powerful Unifying ethic where all members
  maintain this active commitment to the best in each other.

Of course, what makes a huge difference is when parents choose
to focus on the character, unique potential, and destiny of their
children while practicing patience and awareness of the above
three principles: challenge, respect, excellence.

Nationally today, I believe parents need to step up in helping
children find their true selves. Someday the Internet will become
a very powerful educational concept, but now, in its infancy, it
does far more harm than good to the entire youth culture.

I believe this stepping up requires from parents a new dedication in child-rearing. The family has lost its support system and no
longer centers on raising children of character; at the same time,
the school remains too focused on academic proficiency.

A true family-school partnership would empower both, while
giving individual youngsters the support they desperately need.

*And when man faces destiny, destiny ends and man comes into his
own.* —Andre Malraux

Finally, the pursuit of our unique potential and destiny commits
our life to fulfilling a larger purpose, and when that commitment is
maintained, all in the community—family and school—live meaningful lives.

2

CHARACTER

The Unique Potential Creator

As we effectively develop our unique potential, a natural, even instinctual path to our destiny seems to emerge. So the critical question becomes: How do we develop our unique potential? The answer is by making *character development* the moving force of all our efforts.

Education has for its object the formation of character.
—Herbert Spencer

The Greek philosopher Heraclitus even declared, "Character is destiny." By drawing out the deeper character qualities and traits of a young person, we set in motion a powerful *natural process* that propels him or her in the right direction. Take care of character, and unique potential and destiny will follow, as night follows day.

However, it needs to be emphasized that deeper character qualities, such as respect and responsibility, initiate this process. While qualities like curiosity, courage, and integrity help students

The Hyde School, Bath, Maine: A View of the Mansion from the Sunken Garden Where Hyde Graduations Are Held. *Hyde School*

connect to their unique potential, the choices they make in adolescence create additional qualities like generosity and trustworthiness that serve both society and their unique destinies.

We need to emphasize here that destiny is not something dictated by someone else or even by ourselves. Destiny reflects the result of our wide and deep set of potentials, as they are shaped by our parenting, education, and life experience. Our character guides us on the right path and our conscience understands how this equation will ultimately be solved.

The most common commodity in this country is unrealized potential.
—Calvin Coolidge

In character development, parents are the primary teachers and the home the primary classroom. So a successful character process begins at home.

And since life is deliberately difficult in order to bring out the best in us, parents must ensure their character efforts challenge the best in their children so they will become truly capable of coping with life once they reach adulthood. Schools should join parents in these efforts.

The roots of true achievement lie in the will to become the best that you can become.—Harold Taylor

Character cannot be developed in ease and quiet. Only through the experience of trial and suffering can the soul be strengthened, ambition inspired, and success achieved. —Helen Keller

Some might wonder: If this challenge of character development is to fulfill one's destiny, why not just ignore it and enjoy life as it comes?

Hopefully, they would research their doubts. What they would find is that people who pursued a purpose in life were far more fulfilled than those who didn't. And the most fulfilled were those who did it by expressing their deepest potentials—which reflects what we call destiny.

Webster's Dictionary defines "destiny" as "Something that is to happen or has happened to a particular person or thing . . . the predetermined, usually inevitable or irresistible, course of events."

The importance of destiny has been recognized throughout the ages. Johann von Goethe saw destiny in deep spiritual terms: "Life is the childhood of our immortality." Nobel Prize winner Alexis Carrel wrote in his book *Reflections on Life* (published posthumously in 1952), "The first duty of society is to give each of its members the possibility of fulfilling his destiny. When it becomes incapable of performing this duty, it must be transformed."

John W. Gardner, one of the twentieth century's leading scholars, said, "I am entirely certain that twenty years from now we will look back at education as it is practiced in most schools today and wonder that we could have tolerated anything so primitive."

So what is character?

We see a duality in its definition: (1) those *inner* traits that seem to describe our own uniqueness, and (2) those *outer* qualities that seem to describe our worth in the eyes of others. Character balances being true to ourselves with making a contribution to others.

Maintaining this dual definition keeps our Unifying efforts from the two unworkable extremes: letting kids "do their own thing," or just indoctrinating kids into "good" behavior. Educational history has clearly recorded the failure of these two superficial approaches.

The outer qualities of our character define our humanness. Clearly there are universal qualities of character we all share. Some version of the Golden Rule—"Do unto others as you would have them do unto you"—is practiced by every society. We live by laws and rituals, like honoring the dead. We seek cleanliness and respect for our persona. We take our lives seriously.

The same is true for less immediately visible qualities like honesty, respect, responsibility, accountability, citizenship, empathy, dedication, helpfulness, honor, steadfastness, and so on. As concerned parents and teachers, we must help growing youngsters appreciate and internalize these human qualities in order to become fully functioning and effective individuals.

Unless these outer qualities become rooted in the strongest human motivation—the *inner* drive for self-discovery—they will carry limited meaning and permanency to growing youngsters. We have found that certain character qualities (to be discussed) truly inspire the self-discovery process in youngsters and therefore motivate them at a deep level. In time this development leads students to an internalized appreciation for character, and thus also motivates them to acquire additional qualities.

However, our character efforts must always remind students that "you are whatever your unique potential says you are." With so much pressure from today's image-driven society, young people must learn that their ultimate destiny comes from a well-disciplined discovery process of their inner selves. We should continually reassure them of our dedication to help them become the very best they can be, not turn them into what society or others might want them to be.

A CAUTIONARY NOTE ON TEACHING YOUNG PEOPLE

Adults have a natural experiential connection that enables them to teach youth how to live: "Been there; done that." But the link is seldom in use today. To realize this disconnection, note the often negative power of youth culture and peer pressure.

The infant coming out of the womb immediately experiences fear of abandonment. So it seeks to imitate its caretaker, feeling if it is like its caretaker, the caretaker will love it and always be there for it.

This imitation process continues throughout childhood, reflected in sayings like "The apple doesn't fall far from the tree" and "Like father, like son." Regardless of what we may say to them, children learn by imitating us. They develop primarily a visual and instinctual, not a vocal, connection to caretakers: children learn to read our hearts (emotions), not our minds. This is why children are able to manipulate parents. While parents *think* they make a decision on disciplining a child, the child "hears" what the parent will ultimately actually do if the child screws up again, which is often not what the parent threatens.

To be effective, parents—and adults in general—primarily need to learn to raise children by becoming living examples of growth.

Since children read our hearts, our words and actions must be based on our beliefs and character, particularly our honesty about our strengths, challenges, and shortcomings.

Remember, our children have already internalized these things. By consciously sharing them, our strengths give youngsters confidence, and our challenges and shortcomings bring integrity. Parents and children also begin to help each other, particularly with negative dispositions that both internalized in early childhood from parents (more on this in chapter 5).

Finally, adults need to realize that children face a transformational challenge in order to become fully functioning adults.

Their childhood has naturally been focused on them personally, and thus fed their lesser, self-regarding emotions, emphasizing their likes and dislikes, desires and fears. But life will ultimately reward their self-transcending emotions, which define their higher self, valuing such things as truth, beauty, excellence, respect for others, noble deeds, love, destiny.

How this transformation is made varies from child to child. It involves, on one hand, learning to discipline one's lesser, self-regarding emotions, and, on the other hand, reaching beyond them to find one's higher self. Those who do, in fact, make this character transformation live very meaningful and fulfilling lives.

By constant self-discipline and self-control you can develop greatness of character. —Grenville Kleiser

THE UNIFYING FIVE WORDS

Any effective definition of character must first carry a deeper meaning to the students themselves, which is essential to motivating them at their most sustaining levels. We have found this deeper meaning to be embodied in what we call the Five Words: Curiosity, Courage, Concern, Leadership, and Integrity. Perhaps the acid test of their worth is that Hyde graduates come to believe in these qualities even more strongly once they enter life on their own. Here is how the Five Words fit into the development of our unique potential:

- Curiosity: *I am a learner.* Curiosity expresses our dedication to explore life and learning. It drives us to reach beyond ourselves to find our larger purpose in life.
- Courage: *I learn the most about myself by accepting challenges.* Courage is the foundation of individuality. We need it to meet the demands that draw out our unique potential.
- Concern: *I need a challenging and supportive community to develop my character.* Concern expresses our commitment to the welfare of others. "No man is an island"; the destiny of others is ultimately connected to our own.
- Leadership: *I am a leader by asking the best of myself and others.* Leadership expresses our share of making the school and the community—as well as our home life—work at its best. It is the giving of our unique potential to help people and make the world a better place.
- Integrity: *I am gifted with a unique potential, and conscience is my guide in discovering it.* Integrity is the quality of being ourselves in all situations and with all people. It is what truly connects us to our unique potential and destiny.

HOW CHARACTER IS DEVELOPED

Two overriding principles govern the development of character. First, it is primarily learned *by example*. Character isn't really taught; it is caught. We develop character in young people as we develop our own. Teachers and parents must maintain a primary concern for the development of their own character en route to fulfilling their own unique potential and destiny. When teachers and parents take this personal development in themselves and in each other very seriously, youngsters follow their example.

Students come to deeply trust elders they see struggling like themselves with issues of growth, and it gives them confidence that the overall Unifying process of self-discovery and growth is for real. In a Unified community we are all students; some of us are simply older than others. A school environment should feel this vitality of growth.

The second critical principle: in character development, *parents* are the primary teachers and *home* the primary classroom. School programs in character have continually failed because they have never learned how to build on this basic principle. If the goal is to help students develop their unique potential and character, then the staff must fully realize that *the family*, not the school, is the core educational unit. To make a real difference in the lives of students, a school must seek to make a real difference in their families.

The school's Unifying process goes deep; the family goes deeper. The family and school must operate like a team. Unifying teachers must develop a deep understanding of their students, and know they cannot really understand a student at this level until they come to understand the student's parents and home situation.

This school-family bond will elevate character to the primary place in the school's curriculum. It will reaffirm the teacher's efforts, and further help parents examine their efforts in the home. Without this bond, character programs in school will become little more than behavior modifications that kids may discard once they leave school.

If the school makes a real effort to connect to a parent and that effort is rebuffed, the student understands the situation and at least inwardly respects the school's efforts. That at least opens the door to an effective school-student relationship.

It may appear to some that this family-school partnership is just too difficult. But any serious attempt to create it will pay important dividends to the school culture.

CHARACTER: TEACHING AND LEARNING EXAMPLES

Unified students and teachers journal on a regular basis, and often write vignettes or short descriptions about their experiences in the Unifying process. (In chapter 9, we address the family program.) Here are some examples of students learning about character and themselves.

Curiosity

Every day in English, Mrs. B presents us with our own in-depth explanation of the homework. She encourages us to call her at home if we need more explanation or help. She puts together optional evening classes for students who are strug-gling or need a review. She gets so excited in class . . . some-times her voice even cracks. It is this passion and spirit that make me feel obligated to return the favor, not to mention how much I look forward to her class every day.

Mr. G really gets into biology class, and has a love for what he teaches. He takes his class outside, and decorates his classroom like a forest. He understands his students from observing and from spending time with them, in and out of class. He knows how hard students have tried when he reads their exams. He will take time to talk about the individual problems of students. However, he has a strict class and gets a lot of work done.

The one thing Mr. C, Mr. H, and Mr. D all do is keep the class involved. They never let someone slip. They don't call on people to embarrass them, but to see what they think. They look for a student comment to initiate the whirl of energy. They catch you before you fade out. If they see confusion in you, they call on you. If they see excitement, they call on you and encourage it. They have an ability to read their class and what the class needs at that time. Their energy is contagious.

Courage

I had been out of cross-country for about seven weeks with an injured ankle. But when the MSAD [Maine School Administrative District] championships came, I decided I wanted to run for my team. I came in crying and limping, but actually did really well. Mr. G told me that I had shown courage and that he was proud of me.

In soccer my first year, I think the whole team had a problem with courage. Mr. D made us do diving headers all the way across the field. It soon became a regular exercise. It forced us to deal with our courage issues, and Mr. D would not let us give up.

I was struggling with courage to tell my mother the truth about my past. Mr. B said he wouldn't make me tell her, but he was committed to my best. . . . Finally, the three of us spoke about it and my relationship with my mother grew stronger and had a deeper meaning. I know I need courage to deal with the truth with others and within myself.

Concern

I didn't understand why Mrs. B had me read Dreaming in Cuban *over a Thanksgiving break. But I did and I finished it. The young woman in the book struggled with identity and family ties. I am adopted and could relate directly to the character. It was a warm and wonderful feeling to know my teacher had that concern for me, and that she took the time to select something meaningful.*

In biology, Mr. G always puts our plans aside to deal with people and their attitudes. It made the class come together and we learned to work without always using the teacher. I've seen Mr. G stop his entire biology class to deal with a single student who expressed a bad attitude toward her work group. In the end this concern makes the class run much smoother.

Mr. R not only teaches us geometry, he also teaches character. He shows his concern for students by giving them time in and out of the classroom. One time he drove an hour to Lewiston to visit me in the hospital, and brought his son with him.

Leadership

In history, Mrs. B lets students run the class, but she's always in control. She lets us speak our minds and really listens to new ideas. She is open and willing to learn. She admits it when she doesn't know something. She also pushes people to speak up to give them confidence. People are not laughed at for a stupid comment or wrong answer.

Mr. S in algebra has an organized schedule: We know a week in advance what is expected; a student teaches every day, and we are organized in groups of eight which meet twice a week to help each other. It really works if you follow through with everything; by then everything should be understood or else you get a tutor. He expects us to learn the subject well enough to teach the rest of the class.

In English, these are the techniques I observe in Mr. C: (1) He puts the responsibility fully in your lap. (2) He asks you as many questions as possible to get to the root of the problem. (3) He is calm, collected, and relaxed. (4) If there is something he feels he can't handle, he knows how to ask for help. (5) He minimizes the issue by putting it in terms of the future. I have a tendency to magnify or dramatize my role; what Mr. C does, very bluntly and straightforwardly, is to present himself as a mirror that reflects my attitudes and behavior.

Integrity

When I read my autobiography to Mrs. G's English class, I realized it was the truth and that my life was on four sheets of paper. It was a very humbling experience, which showed me the root of many of my hidden attitudes. Most of my problems stem from my childhood and I always had had difficulty looking there before.

This summer Ms. J confronted me about something I really hadn't noticed about myself. Looking back, I could see many instances in which I acted like it was society's duty to bend over backwards for me. I adjusted the rules for my own convenience, never considering the effects these changes might make on other people. Ms. J was someone I confided in and she knew me pretty well. So I took her confrontation to heart. She asked me, "Why are you the exception to the rule?" This took me back and it hurt. But the more I thought about it, the more truth I saw in it. I'm grateful.

I had to get up in front of my English class to present my personal project dealing with "passion and pain." I was at a loss as to exactly what my passion and pain was. After talking to Ms. H, I came to the conclusion that I did have a co-dependency issue. I wrote a story and a few days later, I got up in front of the class and presented it. Halfway through I stopped, and it hit me how strongly this issue affected me—I was partly embarrassed and started to cry. Later, it turned out others shared this problem, too. Overall, it gave me a greater sense of myself and self-confidence.

As students experience the Five Words in the Hyde process, they increasingly focus their development on their own growth and unique potential, hopefully both at home and at school.

3

THE UNIFYING FIVE PRINCIPLES

Guiding the Process

The first step in creating a Unified School Community is to confirm the personal commitments of all participating teachers, staff, parents-guardians, and students. Under the leadership of the school head (principal) and faculty, this teacher-parent-student team commits to creating a strong educational environment with these vital qualities:

- An overriding focus on the development of unique potential and destiny
- A curriculum that draws out Courage, Integrity, Concern for others, Curiosity, and Leadership
- A family-school partnership in which parents are recognized and supported as primary teachers with the home a primary classroom
- A community in which adults lead by personal example and students themselves take a leadership responsibility for each other's best

These directives pose a dramatic, even revolutionary educational challenge. They challenge our creative powers and often require us to "reprogram" some of our past experience and habits. Just as we may continually battle a forest that will seek to reclaim any newly formed clearing, we seek ways to protect our pioneering vision from being overwhelmed by traditional mindsets. This requires the unified effort of Hyde parents, teachers, and students to instill new and supportive mindsets into our School Community. Experience has taught us that individual expressions of the Unifying Five Principles—Destiny, Humility, Conscience, Truth, and Brother's/Sister's Keeper—will form the strong and self-sustaining roots of this new educational culture.

Imagine a community in which all individuals actively share and live by these principles on a daily basis:

- Destiny: *We are gifted with a unique potential that defines a destiny.* This expresses our dedication to making a difference in the world.
- Humility: *We trust in a power and a purpose beyond ourselves.* We gain strength by believing we are part of something larger than ourselves.
- Conscience: *We achieve our best through character and conscience.* Conscience gives us the courage to speak our mind, our heart, and our truth.
- Truth: *Truth is our primary guide.* Truth is our commitment to being honest in both word and deed.
- Brother's/Sister's Keeper: *We help others achieve their best.* Our deepest friendships are built by our commitment to each other's best.

Note that the Unifying Five Words (chapter 2) are "I" concepts and the Unifying Five Principles are "we" concepts. The principles resulted from a year's work (1987–88) of a Hyde group determined to figure out what made the Unifying process work.

The conclusion was that when members of a community sought to live up to the Five Principles, a culture was created that strongly supported each member's character, unique potential, and destiny.

Now apply the Five Principles to the family. Clearly, if all family members accept these principles, it becomes a bond and a powerful culture for growth, including the development of character, unique potential, and destiny.

Character development is the primary means to prepare children for life. It is focused on drawing out their unique potential. Our character efforts with children must always retain this focus, and not fall into the trap of emphasizing behavior traits that simply make us proud of them. Our children were not meant to be part of our trophy case; character growth is always for their sakes, never for ours. If our character-building efforts can maintain this focus on unique potential, we ensure our children will eventually be led by their own conscience.

Teaching students how to hear their conscience and then be led by it is an ultimate goal of parenting and the Unifying process.

UNIFYING PRINCIPLES: TEACHING AND LEARNING EXAMPLES

Here are some vignettes and additional points that describe how adults, especially faculty, begin to inspire students with the Unifying Five Principles.

Destiny

*What was so special about Mr. J was he always believed in me.
He would throw me out of class, make me run laps on the field
for goofing off, and would consistently sit me down and ask
what's going on with me. He always saw a future in me, even
though I was heading downhill. The act of "believing and trusting in an individual" is what he did with me, and it paid off.*

*Mr. I often pulled me over after class and told me I was doing
well, doing great, or doing excellent work. My grades were
actually in the C+ range, but I was struggling and trying my
hardest. His positive comments helped me gain more self-confidence in math. It made me feel good, because in my previous
school my teachers were constantly telling me I was doing hor-
ribly, yelling at me, or making me stay extra hours of detention.*

*Mr. H teaches us we will not understand the government and
its importance until we understand what self-governance is all
about. When I walk into his class I am prepared to feel intense
about what I am going to learn. He makes each of us feel we
can actually do something in our future to make a change. His
knowledge and dedication inspires seniors to have a vision for
themselves and others in life.*

Clearly the concept of destiny requires us to believe in something
beyond ourselves. It maintains in us that crucial humbleness that
is so necessary in child-rearing—that our children are not really
our children, to paraphrase Kahlil Gibran. Our biggest parenting
problem today is our desire to *control*, which simply invites children to seek an unproductive power in response.

The concept of destiny creates its own growth system. Heraclitus's notation that "character is destiny" summarizes why ancient
Greek education was focused on an *inner* search: "Know thyself."

When parents emphasize the development of one's unique potential, children come to realize they won't find their true future through the outside glitter of money or fame, but rather by fully developing the best within themselves, which becomes their character.

Humility

When I was cut from varsity basketball I had to deal with my humility, because I knew I was good enough to make the team. Being cut made me look at my attitude and ego. I struggled dealing with the fact that I had failed. Then I raised my standards, matured as an athlete, and it turned out to be my best year of basketball, because I was forced to take a bigger role on JV. My success on the court led to success in my classes.

Mr. S came into chemistry class one day and shared something personal about himself. I respected him and felt closer to him because of his step of courage. He showed that he trusted us and that we could trust him. From that time on, I had no problem asking for help or holding back any questions I had.

In Ms. H's first year of teaching English, our entire class was struggling. She did not look at it as something we were doing wrong; she involved herself and tried to see what she could do differently. Once we were discussing a scene in a play and she was looking for an answer from one of us, so I said something. Then she got very excited; it was a lot deeper than what she was thinking. She was willing for us to teach her; now we are willing for her to teach us.

Our humility can keep us from abusing our powerful authority with children. It leads us to believe that a higher power than ourselves retains the ultimate responsibility and authority over our children's lives. Humility will also stop us from abdicating our authority in difficult situations with children. We recognize that a deeper, higher power expects us to give our children our very best leadership, even when children or others don't understand our efforts.

Humility becomes a crucial discipline to help parents learn just where their efforts to improve or change their children should end. Just like a skillful surgeon knows where to and where not to use the scalpel, parents' humility helps guide their reverence for their child's uniqueness. It is this skill that leads children to trust parents at the deepest level. It tells children to stop naively seeing their parents as simply the ultimate authority in their lives, and to start listening to them as their primary guidance counselors or mentors. This more mature parent-child relationship is critical to the full realization of the child's unique potential.

Conscience

> When I spent a week on Seguin Island with Mr. R, we worked hard, and I put a lot of hard thinking into the journaling and seminars. Mr. R ran a really tight ship and expected nothing less than our best. He trusted us and was a great role model. When he confronted the group on finding a cigarette butt, I broke down and turned myself in, and then everyone else followed suit. This one moment of conscience will always make me feel good about myself.

> When I was turned in during a bust, I was put in a room with a pencil and paper and told I wasn't coming out until I wrote down what I had done. I was racking my brain trying to remember what it might be (it turned out to be something I had already turned myself in for). Then I remembered returning

from spring break and having a beer with a girl next to me on the plane. Nobody knew about this, so I had the option to get away with it. But I wrote it down and immediately felt better; it didn't even bother me that I would end up on 2-4. I was dealing with a mistake and getting over with it so I could move on.

I hadn't wanted to tell my father that I had lost the plane tickets, because I knew they were expensive. Finally, my conscience was killing me. So I told him how I had lied and that I had lost both plane tickets. He said, "I forgive you for what you did. Do you forgive yourself?"

Just as we believe nature has endowed parents with deep instincts with which to raise children, so has she gifted children with a conscience, which we define as the compass to one's destiny. So as we teach children to challenge themselves, they begin thinking and feeling at a deeper level, which leads them to know themselves and become who they truly are. In time this process can connect youngsters to their conscience—the guidance system for the rest of their lives.

Truth

After I had lied to my English class about doing my homework (I had not), when they questioned me I realized they could see right through me. I finally admitted I hadn't done my homework. It was not only a relief to tell the truth, but I also realized how I had shattered our trust by lying.

When I went on the beach walk with my father, I told him everything I had ever stolen, did, or lied about. I never felt so good about myself, and about my courage and integrity.

*Once, after I turned myself in for breaking ethics, I went to tell
my coach, Mr. B. He told me not to dwell on the past, that it's
not the mistakes you make, it's how you deal with them.*

Truth is the cement that holds families and other groups together.
We may disagree over the nature of a higher power, or argue over
the priority of certain values, but we all accept truth as life's ultimate guide. Our beliefs may or may not be correct, but the truth is
the truth, whether we believe it or not. Organizations that maintain truth as their "higher power" create a deep bond that will hold
their members together.

Of course truth is not the only value; to blurt out the truth in
every situation shows little judgment or discrimination. We must
learn to rely on conscience to dictate what to say or not to say in a
given situation. A good rule of thumb is when in doubt, bet on the
truth.

We will inevitably misperceive the truth at times; we all make
mistakes. But always giving children our *best* perception of the
truth expresses our love and concern, and allows them to trust us
at the deepest level. If we are concerned about our children's
attitudes, or suspect them of something, we should tell them so. If
we are right, then we have put the responsibility for change where
it belongs. If our concerns or suspicions are off target, then we
clear the air, and either we ourselves must make some changes, or
the relationship itself needs to be examined.

There is a deep drive in students, a drive that seeks truth and
honesty in order to build integrity.

Brother's/Sister's Keeper

*At a school meeting, during my first year at Hyde, I got caught
for doing drugs. At first I lied . . . but then people stood up and*

turned me in. *The headmaster asked me where I had gotten the drugs and I lied straight to his face three times in a row, because the person I had gotten them from hadn't been turned in yet, and further, I didn't believe in Brother's Keeper. So I told the school I had gotten them from my little sister back home. This whole experience was a slap in the face, because I realized I didn't care much about myself. I was willing to put both my and my family's reputation, as well as my relationship with my sister, on the line for some girl I was hardly friends with, because I didn't want to be a narc. In his office, Mr. G didn't say a word to me, just let me sit there with what I had done, which was even harder than if he had yelled at me. This experience started me on the right path.*

In seminars at our outpost experience in summer school, I felt a bond with the other people I was with. I found I wasn't the only person who had the feelings I had. For most of my life I thought my feelings were outrageous and alone.

Last January I didn't want to be here. I moped around the school and my spirit seemed to be missing. I was having a hard time in wrestling, consistently losing matches that I should have won. My confidence was low, and I seemed to be betting on my fears. Then in a concern meeting with faculty and students, they told me how they perceived my spirit to be dying, and that I was not doing the Hyde process. Since my way was not working, they suggested I trust what they were saying, and they put me on work crew. During work crew I went to seminars full of emotion and poured out how scared I was. I started to look at myself and, from there, my life took a more positive direction, and I ultimately became the New England Class A champion in my wrestling class.

The fundamental purpose of family is to help children discover and develop their unique potential, which is their connection to their destiny. Until the end of adolescence—which we define as age nineteen—parents must consider their children's growth as their major responsibility in life. This primary focus will help parents deal effectively with their own personal issues in a way supportive to their child-rearing. When parents become too preoccupied with marital or career problems, the growth of both parent and child will suffer. Nature dictates very careful priorities for child-rearing that require our continual respect.

We must always demand the best in our students and children, which, of course, can only be accomplished by always demanding the best from ourselves.

The first prerequisite for healthy and productive children is a deep and even spiritual reverence for always doing one's best. While children may sometimes moan and groan about our relentlessness in this regard, at a deeper level they become reassured by such insistence, because they know—at least unconsciously—that their best is nature's price tag for their ultimate fulfillment. In time, if we so teach them, they will learn to expect the best out of themselves, and even extend it to their siblings and their friends. This is why we call this principle of concern Brother's/Sister's Keeper—and why the most powerful teachers in the Hyde School Community are the students themselves.

Down deep, youngsters believe in the Brother's/Sister's Keeper concept of being responsible for each other, but they come to us from environments that teach them it is an unworkable ideal. So it initially has to be established almost student by student, until a critical mass is reached (roughly 30 percent), at which point the principle becomes accepted by the entire community—just as it took 30 percent of the colonists to create our nation.

✿ ✿ ✿

These are just some examples of the vision, values, and character that the Five Principles inspire. If even just a dedicated minority of teachers, parents, and students seriously practice these principles, they will ultimately create a dynamic culture that will prepare children to live meaningful and fulfilling lives.

Never doubt that a small group of thoughtful, committed citizens can change the world; indeed, it's the only thing that ever has.
—Margaret Mead

PARENTS AND PRINCIPLES

The extent to which parents decide to commit these principles to family life could have a major impact on students in school. The same is true of teachers. It would help them make the practice of the principles in their teaching and in their own lives consistent with that of Unifying students' homes and families. This would both encourage and strengthen the powerful United school-family bond.

A very powerful natural process governs the art of child-rearing. We have found that successful parents raise children with clear principles that help define and reaffirm this natural process of commitment to our best. Let me list just three reasons.

First, letting principles be the final authority helps to avoid unnecessary power struggles with growing children. Kids are constantly testing limits to determine their capabilities, so they inevitably test parents who must impose such limits. However, even the best parents will sometimes be inconsistent or wrong, which invites any kid with spirit to challenge parental boundaries. But principles will be the same tomorrow as they are today, which allows kids to question *interpretation* of a principle, not the parent. Kids can then accept parental authority without feeling they are just giving in.

Second, emphasizing principles is a faster way to help kids become responsible for their own growth. When we parent "out of our heads," the burden is on us to create rules our children can follow; but principles help shift this responsibility to youngsters, who learn to interpret the principles—use their conscience—in order to determine for themselves what actions and behavior are right or acceptable in various situations.

Third, the leadership of principles practically forces parents to raise children effectively. The only true way we teach our children is by example. Principles make us practice what we preach, and therefore they become the means for children to understand our actions in a deeper way, a way they can apply to their own lives. Principles establish strong families.

The concept of unique potential immediately establishes a larger purpose for all of our child-rearing efforts, one that our children can understand and have confidence in. It is a vital step in bonding the efforts of parents, children, and others. It is also a vision that excites children, and thus reaches their deeper spirit and motivation.

This premise begins an important and far-reaching discipline for parenting efforts. It is a constant reminder to parents that their children are also distinct and unique entities who are destined to follow a different path. It further reminds parents to constantly attend to the development of character needed to fulfill their own unique potential and destiny, thus creating the models that will become the foundation of their children's learning. It clearly establishes the basic purpose of the family, which helps to keep children's growth from getting distracted or caught in the powerful dynamics (or dysfunctions) of family life.

The destiny principle, and its belief that every one of us has an important purpose in life, instills a true respect for all individuals, regardless of differences in appearances, beliefs, attitudes, and behavior. It is also the foundation on which youngsters build a deep belief in themselves, while helping them avoid the glamour of images designed to please their peers or to satisfy their short-term wants.

We adults are imperfect; so it is vital that our principles always take precedence in our parenting.

One morning when my son Malcolm was about three, I was late for class. He had crawled into bed with his mother and was watching me frantically trying to get dressed. I couldn't find what I wanted and was becoming more frustrated by the minute. When I opened the drawer filled with socks, none of which matched, I finally exploded. I started angrily throwing them on the floor: "I wish [throw] I had [throw] two socks [throw] that matched!" Whereupon Mal blurted out, "If you act that way about it, you won't get any!" Blanche threw the sheet up over her head, and I stood there like a chastened child.

This story highlights that even at this early age, children are capable of seeing beyond our dominant parent personalities to grasp our principles and values. Parents are the most powerful authority in children's lives. Since we cannot abdicate this authority, it becomes vital to teach our kids that our principles, and not we ourselves, are the ultimate authority.

Finally, if principles offer us such a superior way to raise children, why haven't they become the foundation for all parenting? Because the principles seem too perfect and we are too human. We may believe in them today and then doubt tomorrow. We become frustrated with their intangibility. We become distracted by other problems. We give in to complacency. We pursue temporary child-rearing ideas. The list is endless.

But whatever the difficulty, our principles profoundly influence the growth of our children. In 1963 I turned down a headmastership I deeply wanted because the school resisted integration. While I didn't think much about this decision at the time, I later discovered it had deeply affected nine-year-old Malcolm, who wrote about it in his twenties:

> *Right after returning from Florida, Mom and Dad had one of those "serious" conversations in the living room. Their expressions told me we wouldn't be moving, at least to Florida. I heard them using some big-sounding words. The word that stood out was "segregated"—the reason Dad had refused the job. I was so proud of my father for refusing to work at a school that wouldn't admit blacks, I bragged about it to all my friends. I didn't know if they understood my enthusiasm, but I didn't really care. Perhaps my father believed all of this slipped over my head or perhaps he didn't view it as a major decision on his part. But I needed that example. I had liked being the son of the head coach, teacher, administrator, but that image had a hollow ring. It was his losing the Florida job that gave me something I could really understand, look up to, and follow.*

The challenge for the Unifying teacher is to express the Five Principles in his or her teaching and personal life in a way that supports similar efforts being made by parents. This work will then help solidify the powerful school-family bond, and reassure students of the importance of the Unifying process and family values in their own lives.

In my case, today those principles have woven a strongly united family, with both grown children and grandchildren respecting elders who have dealt and are dealing with imperfections and destinies, just as the younger set are in their lives.

4

THE UNIFYING CULTURE

Roles and Responsibilities

While some public schools have been able to transform their school cultures using Unifying Discovery Groups involving only students and teachers, but not parents, we urge schools to accept the challenge of including parents as described here. Beyond developing a more powerful culture, the ultimate influence on the school and on graduates' lives can be profound.

I use the word "profound" because it was the result of a search I began in 1962 to find a better way to prepare students for life. At a New Year's Eve party, I suffered a crisis of conscience when I realized that the coaching, teaching, and administrating I loved was not in my students' best interests; there had to be a better way to prepare them for life, and that night tagged me to find it.

I became a headmaster in 1964 and began a new program that showed real promise. But I soon discovered I was envisioning change beyond what the trustees would accept. Rather than compromise the program, I resigned after my first year.

The Headmaster Speaks to a Unifying Charter School Student. *Hyde School*

And in spite of lacking the necessary experience and resources, I set out to found a new school, because conscience can generate a very powerful commitment.

As mountain climber W. H. Murray put it:

> Concerning all acts of initiative (and creation), there is one elementary truth, the ignorance of which kills countless ideas and splendid plans: that the moment one definitely commits oneself, then Providence moves too. All sorts of things occur to help one that would never otherwise have occurred. A whole stream of events issues from the decision, raising in one's favor all manner of unforeseen incidents and meetings and material assistance, which no man could have dreamt would come his way. I have learned a deep respect for one of Goethe's couplets: "Whatever you can do, or dream you can do, begin it. Boldness has genius, power, and magic in it."

Perhaps it conveys my commitment that founding Hyde School took four offers to buy the Hyde estate; my first three offers were summarily rejected by the organization that owned the property. As Murray implies, it magically came together in 1966 after my third offer completely fell apart with a price set far beyond my means.

So why this important family involvement in Hyde? It certainly wasn't planned. But in tracing the progress of Hyde graduates in life by 1974, I found that their strongest influence was not Hyde, but their parents. So it became clear to me if I really wanted to help prepare our students for life, we should begin by helping their parents.

Character was central to our learning process, and as we then learned, *in character development, parents are the primary teachers and home the primary classroom.*

This reality lifts all roles: the parent plays an active and meaningful role, the teacher facilitates, and the student participates.

The roles of our students, teachers, and parents are different and more advanced than those roles in traditional education. To do the Unifying process effectively, the differences need to be fully appreciated.

The Unified culture is the powerful and essential setting for the development of character and unique potential. It creates the cocoon for the transformation from our lesser self to our higher human self. It serves as the crucible that develops students into leaders.

A school culture is defined by its purpose. Whereas the traditional school seeks intellectual proficiency of students, a Unified school seeks their moral as well as their intellectual development. This major difference in purpose creates two entirely different cultures that sometimes lead people to say they experience culture shock when they enter a Unifying culture.

Webster's Dictionary defines "culture" in these ways:

- The act of developing the intellectual and moral faculties, especially by education
- Enlightenment and excellence of taste acquired by intellectual and aesthetic training
- The integration pattern of human knowledge, belief, and behavior that depends upon man's capacity for learning and transmitting knowledge to succeeding generations

Reviewing these definitions, we have to wonder: How, when, and why did traditional education shed the deeper aspects of what defines culture (moral, aesthetic, belief, and behavior) and become narrowly focused on just intellectual development?

Even worse, traditional education sees "intellectual" development as relating only to the mastery of academic subjects in order to meet the requirements of standardized tests, colleges, and employers. The development of curiosity, intellectual character, a love of learning, and other deeper intellectual qualities may occur in traditional schools, but they are the exception and not the rule.

The reduced purpose of traditional education has seriously weakened the culture of American schools, leaving them vulnerable to the dominant popular culture in society, a culture largely driven by commercial interests and the youth market.

In contrast, our purpose of developing the character and unique potential of each student creates a well-defined and powerful culture of its own, which is able to repel outside agendas, no matter how strong. For example, today's image-focused youth culture—what matters most is how you look—seriously compromises the learning environment, but it cannot survive in a Unifying culture. Similarly, the "do your own thing" attitude or "look the other way if you see cheating" stance, both prevalent in the youth cul-

Hyde Elementary Charter School Students. *Hyde School*

ture, won't last when confronted by our Brother's/Sister's Keeper ethic.

Over time, the roles and responsibilities of each member of the Unifying community become very clear, and each person is important to the culture and to the fulfillment of a Unifying culture's purpose, which is one's full preparation for life.

Within a Unifying culture, the head of school is the ultimate authority, not unlike a queen bee, whose most important function is to enforce the social order of the hive. He or she is responsible for ensuring the culture's continual reverence for the development of unique potential, and he or she allows no other concerns or authorities to transcend this reverence. He or she is the spiritual leader of the school, and the caretaker of the integrity of both the Unifying culture and process.

Excellence in growth requires synergy. Recall the kindergartners in Daniel Coyle's study of groups. The five-year-olds, working together with one mind, created a synergy that led to impressive success. Such synergy could be expressed as 1 + 1 = 3.

Since synergy is primarily produced by the culture, every member of the Unifying community is held responsible for practicing two ethics that support its standards.

- No Private Conversations: This ethic helps eliminate hidden agendas, cliques, and interchanges that could erode trust within the community. The "no private conversations" ethic means if A talks to B about C, then A becomes obligated to also tell C, and B is obligated to ensure that happens. Eliminating private conversations allows all concerns and conflicts to be resolved, even if it requires involving the school head. This helps sustain the flow of truth and trust within the culture.

- Humility: This ethic helps to keep egos and authority conflicts from disrupting the vital synergy of the culture. We all maintain certain authorities in our lives, particularly in our families. The Hyde process is bound to challenge the natural authority we have over ourselves and our lives, as well as the authority we reserve for our families. It may require great humility in some situations to allow the Unifying culture to direct change in ourselves and our families.

Successful organizations operate at a high level of trust. Here's an example from my experience: One day at football practice when I was talking to my squad, several kids were apparently horsing around, and before I could say anything, Pete (the quarterback) angrily said, "Knock it off!" A few moments later Pete heard the noise again. Mistakenly blaming Bob, our star lineman, Pete said, "Bob, take a lap!"

As Bob started to protest, Pete cut him off, saying, "Take the lap or get off the field!" My heart was in my throat because, knowing Bob as a quiet but proud individual, I thought the confrontation would cost us both our star player and our QB's leadership. But respecting Pete's leadership, Bob silently took the lap, even though he wasn't to blame. (Not surprisingly, Pete eventually became an outstanding football captain at college, and Bob a highly respected university athletic director.)

I'm sure Pete apologized later to Bob once he learned the truth, but in that moment everything happened so fast that our team unity relied upon Bob's humility.

Of course, we don't just robotically do what we're told. Conscience, not compliance, is the objective. There are times when our individual expressions of conscience are needed to lead the community. But we must be sure that our conscience—and not our ego—does the talking in these critical situations; humility can teach us when and how.

We rely upon the head of school to ensure that practicing these two ethics neither compromises the integrity of Hyde individuals nor compromises the integrity of the Hyde process and culture. Clearly, therefore, much depends upon the character and leadership of the school head. Perhaps the most important function of the Hyde board of governors is to be certain the Hyde culture is always led by such an exceptional individual. Hopefully, school boards employing the Unifying process would do the same.

The "no private conversations" and humility ethics create a synergistic flow and continuity to the process, to the benefit of all.

The Unifying culture creates a revolutionary new relationship between family and school. While the traditional school and family operate as separate, autonomous entities, the best Unified culture requires a genuine school-family integration. This unity radically changes how parents and teachers relate to each other—and how students relate to both.

Parents are the natural authority over children and the family. Parents are also the most influential figures in the Unifying culture. In character development, parents are the primary teachers and home the primary classroom. Thus, within this culture, parental and school authority can easily conflict—even unconsciously.

For example, at Hyde all of us—teachers, students, and parents—are supposed to actively participate in helping parents effectively raise their children, a no-no outside the Hyde culture. At Hyde, excellence in family is a must in achieving excellence in school.

To create a strong culture and cocoon, Hyde parents need to conscientiously and continually support the school's program by example, both at school and at home. Their willingness at times to defer their own authority to the Unifying process serves as a powerful example for children to follow.

Such deference may go against the grain of some parents; entrusting the future of their children to any school may seem irresponsible. But parents have continual opportunities to step back and evaluate whether their trust in the Unifying process is justified.

In essence, they are really being asked to test the process for themselves and their families, not just trust it. The Unifying process recognizes parents and families as the ultimate authority.

Testing the process brings parents closer to internalizing it. When the Unifying process is internalized, it can dramatically improve parental effectiveness, which in turn develops a deeper trust in families. Generally, parents and their children unanimously come to believe that the Unifying process transforms them. Such families then become powerful mentors for other families in our community.

The Hyde board of governors is the ultimate authority of our school. Primarily concerned with the overall management and direction of the school, they maintain an objective oversight position, hiring, assisting, or terminating the school head. They are involved within the Hyde culture only with board chairman and school head consent.

No one within the current Hyde culture serves on the board. However, alumni parents who have internalized the Unifying process—as well as older alumni—form the Hyde board. The board creates its own Unifying culture, and its dedication and overall leadership gains the trust of the Hyde community. So former parents and graduates oversee all Hyde operations.

The purpose of any educational process largely determines teacher, student, and parent roles. Traditional education is narrowly focused on the academic achievement of the student, which puts a premium on the dissemination of knowledge. Its educational process is heavily dependent upon the teacher because the teacher controls both the knowledge and its dissemination. Thus, the teacher's mind centers the educational process, creating a very authoritarian system. The student's role is primarily a reactive one to teacher directives. The parent's role is almost nonexistent.

With its focus on achievement, traditional education motivates students toward getting good grades instead of toward learning, as widespread cheating painfully shows us.

Innate abilities and learning styles play a major role in academic achievement, but traditional education fails to address these individual needs. Many students give up or simply refuse to compete. In addition, since the emphasis on achievement primarily makes students rival competitors, the powerful resource of synergy is largely lost.

Traditional education also assumes the family is establishing a student's character foundation. Generally, students cannot effectively be trained academically if they lack this foundation. There are "gifted" students who seem to achieve academic success without a solid character, but they won't succeed in life if their academic proficiency doesn't also reflect a deeper sense of purpose. That certainly proved true in my 1962 calculus class, which helped lead to my crisis of conscience. I was trying to tell a lazy and self-centered fourteen-year-old genius that his attitude would crucify him in life, but I was giving him my highest grade! Then I tried to get a Vermont farm boy to ignore his feeling—*I work twice as hard as everyone else and get half as much out of it*—and trust that his character would fulfill his goal of becoming a top engineer, but I was giving him my lowest grade!

When I wrote my book *Character First* (1993), my editor asked what happened to those two students. I discovered that the first (poor attitude) had been unemployed for eleven years, in spite of graduating from MIT with an A average, while the second (trusting his character) had won several engineering awards.

Our present educational system has proven ineffective over a long period of time because its students increasingly lack a necessary character foundation. Many students today do not exhibit a sense of purpose regarding academic work; nor are they curious about learning or dedicated to academic excellence. Learning is of minor importance to most students; they instead simply focus on grades for recognition and college entrance.

In fact, this system was designed for an earlier America, a time when the extended family and the community more attentively developed the character and overall growth of children, therefore allowing schools to effectively concentrate on literacy and academics.

Today we face a far more complex world that places greater demands not just on our intellect, but on our emotional and spiritual resources as well. Our schools almost completely ignore these deeper resources, and the cost to human life is tremendous. According to the National Institute of Mental Health, 46.4 percent of adults today will experience mental illness in their lifetime. In essence, our system of education has become a square peg in a round hole. W. Edwards Deming brilliantly inspired both Japanese and US industry by teaching them the monumental difference between problems created by ineffective systems and problems created by ineffective workers.

We Americans have stubbornly related our educational ills to ineffective workers, blaming undisciplined and unmotivated students, underperforming teachers, and uninvolved parents. But Deming recognized that American education has a systems problem: students, teachers, and parents do poorly today because the tools we give them ignore their best. We narrowly focus on the academic prowess of students while largely ignoring their vital character growth.

And we completely ignore the dominant role parents could play. Deming called our educational system "horrible."[1]

The first responsibility of any educational system is to prepare students for life. We seek to build a new educational system, one that truly respects what students, teachers, and parents have to give, and one that unites their efforts in order to rebuild the foundation of character, which will help them all succeed in life.

The Unifying process changes the focus of education from the student's academic growth to a more comprehensive focus on the student's unique potential, which is primarily discovered by developing the student's character.

This new unique potential focus revolutionizes the roles of student, teacher, and parent. The new roles in a nutshell:

- Student: The student "owns" his or her unique potential, so the student and not the teacher is the center in the educa-

tional process. Students need to learn to accept this new
and demanding level of responsibility and accountability.

• Parent: Character is the primary means to discover and develop unique potential, so parents now become the primary
teachers in the educational process and home the primary
classroom. Since character is taught by example, parents
need to develop a significantly higher level of discipline and
structure in their own lives.

• Teacher: Given these student and parent roles, teachers
must learn how to facilitate a new learning process, assisting
students and parents in their new roles. Teachers also need
to lead by example.

The dedication of the Unifying student, parent, and teacher, together with the dedication of a Unifying community, provides a
powerful synergy.

THE UNIFYING STUDENT

In understanding and then meeting the responsibilities of new
roles, we need to realize the huge problem all of us face in trying
to grow beyond the roles we already know and have been trained
to fill. We need courage and dedication to venture beyond them.

The Unifying culture seeks to build a new education that truly
respects what students, teachers, and parents have to give.

As creatures of habit, we have been indoctrinated into how
students, teachers, and parents are supposed to operate. And we
have internalized our present habits far more than we realize. So
even though we may intellectually understand what our new roles
are in the Unifying process, we must realize that it will take a great
deal of practice at a deeper emotional level before we truly begin
to internalize our new responsibilities. (Remember how awkward-

Unifying the School Community Inspires Motivation. *Hyde School*

ly we first rode a bicycle with just our minds, until our body and emotions internalized the learning.)

> *We first make our habits, and then our habits make us.*
> —John Dryden

Unifying Student Role

Students take active responsibility for their own learning and growth. They also learn to take responsibility for the growth of both their peers and the school at large. Teachers and parents work together to maximize the responsibility of students in the learning process.

The price of greatness is responsibility. —Sir Winston Churchill

This should be the obvious first step in any educational process, but it is an absolutely essential first step in the Unifying process, and becomes a continuing major challenge to students, teachers, and parents alike.

Here is one student's story of learning the deeper meaning of integrity:

> *I struggled getting my work done most of the year. I made excuses for myself and convinced myself I was incapable. Then one of my teachers held me after class and told me I lacked integrity because of my helplessness in academics. At first I was defensive and acted like a victim, but shortly after, I realized she was right. By me not holding the same standards for myself in all aspects of my life, I was not living a life of integrity.*

Unifying students take an active responsibility for their own learning and growth.

For example, in traditional education, if the teacher forgets to assign homework, the student has no responsibility to do anything. The student should be responsible to at least ask if there was any homework. In traditional education, a student needs a note signed by an adult to excuse lateness. The Unifying student is responsible for truthfully explaining why he or she is late.

(This first step, students being fully responsible, is very healthy for American child-rearing. In traditional education, both parents and teachers continually pick up responsibilities adolescents could and should be handling.)

To see this more clearly, note that in our society, adolescence is primarily viewed as a time for fun, not as a time in which serious preparation for life needs to occur. The term "teenager" is generally associated with images of irresponsibility and immaturity; such behavior is often expected. This has happened because we have learned to treat teenagers simply as older children, not as the adults-in-progress they actually are.

In terms of what teenagers could and should be, we need to remember the key role many American teenagers played in winning World War II, and then in becoming the highest-performing college students this country has ever seen. Today we refer to them as the Greatest Generation. Their outstanding teenage performance reaffirmed the wisdom of the great psychologist and philosopher William James, who urged in a classic essay in 1910 that our society and growing youngsters needed to be challenged with "the moral equivalent of war" in order to help them realize their deeper character and true sense of identity.

As a wartime teenager, along with experiencing gas, food, and other rationing, I was expected to help keep our "victory garden," to crush cans, and to accomplish other resource-saving tasks to support the war effort. My ten-week navy boot camp experience and later tour were important steps in my growing up. We can construct a powerful crucible of similar challenges and sacrifices to help youngsters today experience the development of their maturity and leadership, war or no war.

The generations of teenagers who followed those of World War II have never been able to match the Greatest Generation's outstanding achievement because they have been stuck in an educational system that treats them like children.

Challenge and adversity must become an integral, positive part of adolescent growth in America. How do we accomplish this? By introducing a new educational process that fully expresses our high expectations for our children's growth and, further, one that offers transformational "crucible" experiences.

The Unifying process gives adolescents and their parents a life-determining choice: continue to trust today's failing educational system to properly prepare for a meaningful and fulfilling life, or seek the deeper challenge and transformational change that the Unifying process offers.

This is a choice that honors the final lines of Robert Frost's famous poem "The Road Not Taken":

> *Two roads diverged in a wood, and I—*
> *I took the one less traveled by,*
> *And that has made all the difference.*

The development of our unique potential requires us to take roads less traveled in life. When I left business (and ignored my ego seeking fame and fortune) to enter teaching, I initially felt humiliation and cursed that my unique potential dictated I should be a teacher. Today I am so thankful I chose my own road less traveled, for I know that teaching is the source of my ultimate fulfillment and contribution in life.

After seventy years of helping kids prepare for life, I am convinced that our unique potential defines both who we are and our true destiny in life, and if we hope to fully discover these forces, we must begin the development of our unique potential in our adolescence.

The more responsibility parents take, the more they will encourage their child to resist acting responsibly. Here is a mom's description of honoring her responsibility to her son's future:

> *My son Mike was not happy at Hyde and wanted to come home and attend his old public high school with all of his friends. His father and I suffered through Mike's first year at Hyde listening to him accuse us of lying to him and how inappropriate*

Hyde was for him. His father and I decided to make our position clear by Christmas of Mike's junior year.

Our message to Mike was that he had the choice to leave Hyde for his senior year, but we would not support him financially. He could go to school with his friends, but needed to find a place to live and a way to put money into his pocket. Mike refused to speak to either of us for all of winter term, not a word. Shortly before the end of the term he called to say that he could not support himself working at McDonald's and once again was being forced to do what we wanted. He was angry and felt manipulated even though I pointed out it was his decision.

Mike did finish and graduate from Hyde. In his graduation speech and letter to me, he thanked me for forcing him to stay at Hyde.

In life, we all must begin to choose between two basic motivations. Option 1: try to control our lives and live them the way we choose. Option 2: seek to realize our unique potential and purpose in life and accept whatever that offers us.

If we are wise, we will come to recognize that Option 1 feeds our initial and lesser instincts of seeking pleasure and avoiding fear, while Option 2 honors our deepest human motivation of self-discovery and fulfillment of a larger purpose.

Helping children develop responsibility and accountability for their own growth—as they (and we) pursue Option 2—should be an essential and continuing priority. Children enter life with zero responsibility for their own growth; they need to be prepared by us to accept the majority responsibility of their lives once they finish their teens.

In the Unifying process, student responsibility—as well as the system of accountability that ensures its continual development—is a primary focus.

Unifying Student Responsibilities

We expect students to take the majority of responsibility for their own growth by graduation. Most of our Bath, Maine, students begin way behind in accepting responsibility, because parents and their previous schools expected so little responsibility from them beyond academic proficiency.

American parents have difficulty letting go of children because they want the best for them and thus often become overly concerned about their children's progress. This leads them to take more responsibility for their children's growth than they should, which in turn lulls their children into taking less responsibility than they should.

Students assume as much of the teaching responsibilities at Hyde as their level of maturity will allow them.

Here a student shares an important step taken during a three-day family seminar, known as a Family Learning Center (FLC), realizing her deeper self by dealing with a parent relationship:

> *I hadn't spoken to my father in six months; he wasn't really a part of my life for sixteen years, so I was ready to totally remove him from my life altogether, until he signed up for an FLC. I was absolutely mortified to have a three-day seminar with him without my mom. At first, my attitude was horrible and my dad seemed to be turning everything around on me. I wasn't getting anything out of it, so I decided to fake my way through it, which didn't get me anywhere either.*
>
> *Then, thanks to my friend, I found the courage to take a huge risk and I told my dad every single thing that was holding me back from having a relationship with him. Since he couldn't deny the things I was saying in front of a larger group, he was forced to take in and really think about what I was saying. With the group's support, he was able to dig deep into his past,*

*and share many things from his childhood, and he found things
he could really work on.*

*We are now working on a trusting and productive relation-
ship that would not have been possible without the FLC.*

Most parents unwittingly become more concerned about their
children's future than their children are. This leads to a pattern
where the more irresponsibly the child acts, the more responsibility the parent accepts.

Parents need to realize that, given their high expectations, children often fear they will fail as adults, and thus will try to hang on
to being children as long as they can. So the more responsibility
parents take, the more they will encourage their children to resist
acting responsibly.

American schools give students minimum responsibilities as
well. Adults run everything at school, a fact that caters to adolescent fears of growing up and helps lull teenagers into remaining
children. It is as if the educational process is geared to accommo-
date the least responsible students.

The student has absolutely no responsibility for classmates,
even to deter or report harmful or criminal behavior.

In contrast, here are some of the expectations of our students:

- To cultivate a curiosity about life and learning, continually
  addressing the three basic questions: *Who am I? Where am I
  going? What do I need to get there?*
- To practice delayed gratification: purpose before pleasure,
  work before play, hard before easy.
- To practice the "never lie–never quit" ethic.
- To practice and honor the Five Words and Five Principles.
- To respect the active input of family members, Hyde staff,
  and Hyde students.

- To demand the best from family members, Hyde staff, and Hyde students.
- To honor the dictates of one's conscience.

What most distinguishes our students is the leadership role they assume in the Unifying process and in the school as expressed in Brother's/Sister's Keeper. Students assume as much of the teaching responsibilities at Hyde as their level of maturity will allow them.

Under the Brother's/Sister's Keeper ethic, they are committed to the best growth of all Hyde community members. It is not unusual for our students to counsel a student, teacher, staff member, or parent. It is well understood that Hyde students can be Hyde's most effective teachers.

Our students are committed to ensuring that Hyde ethics are honored by all community members. To fail to do so is considered a serious compromise of ethics. All students regularly participate in a school-wide evaluation of Hyde teachers, and Hyde teachers have come to appreciate these sessions as a powerful tool in their personal and professional growth.

Here is one young teacher's experience of the student evaluation, part of his job interview:

> I sat down with seven or eight students. I looked up at all the young faces and tried to appear in control of things. My act had always worked before, but there was something different about this scene; I felt uneasy, like they were seeing right through me. Finally, a young man shot out, "So what do you struggle with?"
>
> Not knowing exactly what he was looking for, I gambled a response: "Well, I struggle with family. We've always been close and now that I'm out of college, I feel our relationship should change—that I should become less dependent on par-

ents in making my decisions—but it feels like we're all lost in this maze of the past twenty-two years."

With that confession I looked sheepishly into my plate, but I felt a new relaxation in my body. Then the young man said, "Yeah, I can relate to that. I'm about to head off to college myself. My problem is a little different; I've just started to develop a relationship with my parents and I'm worried college will pull us apart."

For the first time, I felt I was part of my own interview. Later they asked me if I had any questions. Again I gambled: "I understand some students at Hyde have had drug and alcohol problems. I've never experimented with that stuff before and I'm worried I wouldn't be able to relate to those kids."

A student replied, "Dependence, it's all the same thing."

My thoughts spun. I was dumbfounded with admiration for his wisdom and excited for the challenge he presented me. On some level we all struggle with the same things: dependence, escape, fear. Why had I always insisted that somehow I was different?

To develop an effective school program, the Unifying process centers itself on parent and family growth, a major departure from traditional education. Everyone here is both a teacher and a student. The extent to which we exemplify these roles is a reflection of the stage of growth we happen to be experiencing.

THE UNIFYING PARENT

The Hyde parent role is probably the most demanding one in America, if not the world. Our boarding school parents spend a minimum of twelve full days in residence on campus and also spend time in their geography-based "parent regions," focused on their own growth and the growth of their families. They are asked to exemplify the soul-searching dedication that we expect of their Hyde students, and then to continually express what they are learning in their lives, families, and careers.

Hyde parents and their families generally experience a major transformation in their lives.

Unifying Parent Role

Character development is the primary means to discover and develop our unique potential—the purpose of the Hyde process. But in character development, as we have emphasized, parents are the primary teachers and home the primary classroom. So to develop an effective school program, our Unifying process centers itself on parent and family growth, a major departure from traditional education.

We form our character in families, and under parental guidance. As creatures of habit, we carry into our school experience the character foundation we learned at home. The traditional educational experience is seldom deep enough to penetrate this foundation.

When parent character foundation is in sync with our Unifying School program, our deeper human growth becomes reaffirmed. But when character foundation is not in sync, we may need to confront family issues and dynamics that formed the foundation. This in turn may require parents to confront issues, attitudes, and even deeper emotional dispositions that led to their character foundation.

The implication here might seem to be negative—that student character growth issues in school are linked to family and parent character growth issues at home. This is sometimes true, but the larger and more important point is this: parenting excellence and family excellence form the foundation for character excellence. So if a school aspires to achieve excellence of character, it must strive to help those in its community achieve parenting and family excellence.

The Unifying process requires a high level of truth. Here a teacher realizes the need to match personal honesty with professional honesty:

> *I came to teach at Hyde because I agreed deeply with the school's words and principles, and I was certain I lived by those same values. But after sharing my experiences and listening to those of students and faculty, it became clear I was not practicing the same honesty with my family and my wife; I merely avoided uncomfortable topics. The aura of frank discussion and insight into those around you at Hyde helped me see my own misperceptions and manipulations. My willingness to ask for more in my life was the key to using the Hyde process.*

Just as academic excellence requires a continuing excellence in fundamentals like math and English, so does character excellence require a continuing excellence in fundamentals. This means all three excellences—parenting, family, and character growth at school—must be developed in concert. Growth in one inevitably means growth in all three.

If a school aspires to achieve excellence of character, it must strive to achieve parenting and family excellence. The major difficulties in achieving character excellence today are (1) parents and families are not exposed to programs designed to achieve parenting and family excellence, and (2) schools are not exposed to programs designed to achieve character excellence. Hyde seeks excellence in home, school, and community unity.

Unifying Parent Responsibilities

Character is primarily taught by example. Therefore, Hyde parent responsibilities are virtually the same as the student responsibilities, except they are generally practiced by the parent at a more advanced level:

- To cultivate a curiosity about life and learning, continually addressing the three basic questions: *Who am I? Where am I going? What do I need to get there?*
- To practice delayed gratification: purpose before pleasure, work before play, hard before easy.
- To practice the "never lie–never quit" ethic. We elevate the level of truth in our families and ourselves, and inspire our families with our courage.
- To practice and honor Hyde's Five Words and Five Principles. We create a character culture in our homes and bond our families with the Hyde community.
- To respect the active input of family members, Hyde staff, Hyde students, and other Hyde parents in our growth.
- To demand the best from family members, Hyde staff, and Hyde students.
- To honor the dictates of one's conscience.

Parents who successfully meet these responsibilities are leaders and stewards of character growth in society.

Here a parent shares how she began the Unifying process with a dubious attitude but grew to truly appreciate it:

> When first introduced to the Hyde process, I thought the sessions were touchy-feely BS, so I participated grudgingly and skeptically. I thought the sessions were pretty tedious and I didn't enjoy them; I just put in my time.

Then it dawned on me that my son was only a sophomore and that I was looking at three more years of this stuff. How was I going to survive? So I started thinking seriously about my writing assignments. I often found myself very sad and even crying as I wrote. At first I was scared to read this stuff publicly, but I found nothing but support. Occasionally somebody would make a critical comment, and when I started to explain myself further or defend my position, the group wouldn't allow it.

It wasn't until later that I realized the critical comments were usually correct and very helpful. So I started giving my honest feedback to what others said. I found this very difficult when what I had to say was counter to what I thought they wanted to hear. But I've been thanked later by people for giving them honest feedback. It felt good.

As I got more comfortable with the process, I found I didn't think or worry about my son anymore. And the more I focused on myself, the better he got and the closer we became. Now I eagerly await Hyde meetings and find them incredibly refreshing and supportive.

Here a Hyde student notes how the Hyde process is transforming her father into a more effective model and teacher:

Dad, you have recently inspired me through your humility to be open and to learn from other people. I've watched you change from an angry closed person to a humble one. The memory that is especially vivid is the one of you in the parent show wearing a hula skirt and coconut bra. I now have a much greater understanding of the phrase, "Get out of yourself and have some fun." You have shown me what it means to not be afraid of who you are.

THE UNIFYING TEACHER

The student controls the Unifying process, the parent is its primary teacher, and the family its primary classroom. So where does all this leave the Unifying teacher?

As a teacher, when I first realized the parent was and would remain the most influential figure in my students' lives, I felt depressed. I had thought I could reach any kid; but this new realization painfully told me the real effectiveness of my teaching depended upon parents, and that my best would seldom overcome their worst.

But I finally said to myself, "Well, Joe, if you really want to help kids, then help their parents." Once I began helping parents, I soon realized this also meant helping their family. In time the Hyde process introduced me to a powerfully advanced level of

Hyde Coach Prepares His Basketball Team for Another New England Class D Championship. *Hyde School*

teaching, and to an even deeper influence in the lives of my students.

Unifying Teacher Role

I learned that sometimes you help a parent or a family to help a kid, and sometimes you help a kid to help a parent or a family. Often, some of those you help don't even know it. But you yourself know, and in time you realize this knowledge is the ultimate fulfillment for a teacher. You come to appreciate the opportunities for growth you have given all of them, regardless of what they may do with those opportunities.

So with the new Unifying teaching role, the teacher continues to teach students, but at a deeper level of development that includes teaching each student's parents and family. In essence, the Unifying teacher becomes a combination of master teacher, guidance counselor, and facilitator of the process.

Here a Unifying teacher describes the process of learning to confront colleagues and adults as well as students:

> A tough issue for me as a Hyde teacher has been being honest with my colleagues. The big stuff is not an issue; if I have a major concern I will speak openly with my peers. It's the everyday conflicts that test my commitment to Brother's/Sister's Keeper. I let my doubts get in the way. I think, "What will this person think of me? How will they react? This is so petty, I'll just drop it."
>
> I had the job of lining up faculty to go on wilderness trips. I found myself going to a select group—young teachers who were open to this additional responsibility and veterans who would always try to juggle things if you were in a pinch. I knew C would refuse so I put off asking him. Finally, I approached him in the hall. He blurted out, "I don't think I can. I will have

to look at my schedule." We were both uncomfortable with our exchange and we both quickly walked away.

I thought a lot about it later and made an important realization: my fear of C's response was keeping me from my best. It was really more my issue than his. I approached him the next day: "C, I want to call myself on something. I've been second-guessing you and it hasn't been fair. I assumed you would not be open to any additional responsibilities so I have avoided asking you in the past. I'm sorry I prejudged you and I'm going to work on changing that." He looked at me with surprise and then we proceeded to have a deep conversation about his fears.

I learned to handle such situations by focusing upon myself. By using "I" statements rather than "You" statements, I put the emphasis on the positive and allowed C to decide what he needed to look at in this situation.

Unifying Teacher Responsibilities

The Unifying teacher is a remarkable individual and professional. He or she is committed to the development of the character and unique potential of all members of the United community. He or she models the Five Words and Five Principles at an exemplary level.

Here is how one student sees Unifying academics at their best:

This is what I noted in great teaching at Hyde: confidence, appreciation for insight, pushing students further than they think they can go, teaching students things they could never think of on their own, passion about your subject.

The Unifying teacher tries to assume all the responsibilities to both students and parents and seeks to model them at an exemplary level. In terms of rigor, he or she constantly seeks both personal and professional growth at an excellence level. In terms of synergy, he or she appreciates both the criticisms and compliments of students, parents, and colleagues and never hesitates to criticize and compliment all of them. In terms of conscience, he or she consistently seeks the truth.

The traditional emphasis on achievement leads students to feel schools are indoctrinating them, which breeds their distrust. This story from a young Unifying teacher shows skill in helping new students unlearn some of these attitudes:

> At a school meeting, the summer school director passed out photographs of a basketball player who only had one leg, and then read an article about this man who played in the Special Olympics. He obviously had a first-rate attitude and work ethic, was a capable player, and most remarkably seemed utterly lacking in bitterness. The article sparked discussion about determination and how easy it is to take things for granted. It was a good school meeting.

> The next day in class, Ivan started to complain about the meeting: "So the guy's got one leg. So he's brave and tough and all that. Yeah, yeah, yeah. Sure, it's inspiring, but so what? I've heard this stuff a hundred times before . . ." and so on. Ivan's attitude was horrendous; but thinking back to my own experience in public schools, I knew where he was coming from. Instead of jumping down his throat, I decided to turn the incident into a teaching moment.

> We spent the entire class talking about the differences between how most schools work and how Hyde School works. In most schools, the students felt, the teachers had the knowledge and opinions and the students were just there to regurgitate them. The teachers were always trying to plant ideas into the heads of the students rather than encourage them to think for themselves. This was what Ivan was reacting to—thinking the

director was trying to manipulate the students into feeling a certain way, rather than simply sharing a story and then letting them react.

We also explored the idea that if you don't know something, it is a sign of weakness in most schools. Students always wanted to say, "I know the answer" and would be embarrassed to say, "I don't know. Please tell me."

We decided that schools should value "curious inquiry" over "smug knowledge." We also discussed honoring effort over achievement, and finally, having an open mind. Taking a poll of the class, we quickly discovered that those who had listened with an open mind at the school meeting had been energized and inspired by it. Ivan had presupposed the goal, consequently not really listening, and he wound up hating the meeting.

What was wonderful about the class is that students explored what they didn't like about schools, what they did want from their schools, and how a good learning attitude made school rewarding and even fun (a radical concept to some of them).

I remember this class because I had been able to act as a facilitator for learning rather than a dispenser of knowledge. I had invited dissent rather than squelched it, treated students' opinions with respect, and taught to their curiosity, not their knowledge. I try to remember this class so I can continue following this model.

Another story illustrates the need for teachers to respect their own unique potential:

When I began my career as an environmental educator, I was deeply envious of the way my colleague, Tim, could motivate and excite students. His lessons were always full of energy; he could electrify kids and have them hanging on his every word. I remember thinking if I were only half as good, I would be an outstanding teacher.

One day I decided to emulate Tim as best I could. I launched into the lesson with the same passion and enthusiasm Tim exuded. I couldn't believe the student responses. The lesson was a total flop.

I put this experience behind me for several months, but then one evening I opened up to Tim, telling him how deeply I admired him as a teacher, and how envious I was of his teaching. To my surprise he looked me straight in the eyes and said he had always been envious of the way I taught. I was stunned, since I had always considered my lessons vanilla-like. But Tim pointed out my knack for having students conduct serious experimentation and study, something he was never able to do.

Teaching, he said, is not just about exciting students; learning has a discipline that isn't always fun, and he saw my gift as being able to motivate students to this level of learning in a way that didn't turn them off.

Reflecting back now, while we need teaching mentors to help guide our teaching, it is very important each of us develops a teaching style that reflects our own unique potential. I couldn't become a Tim, and Tim couldn't become me. Our discussion convinced me my best teaching will always be a deeper reflection of who I am as a person.

Few things are impossible to diligence and skill. Great works are performed not by strength, but perseverance. —Samuel Johnson

It is vitally important that teachers personally and professionally model the Hyde process for students, just as parents should model their growth for children. This includes being honest and having the courage to seek help.

Here's one teacher's story of her own learning:

I began teaching full of excitement and ideas, but also unsure of myself and lacking in confidence. I stuck closely to what I was comfortable teaching. Then the English department head told me I needed to teach The Merchant of Venice *by Shakespeare, and I immediately looked for ways around it.*

I had always struggled to understand Shakespeare; the truth was he intimidated me, so I avoided his works. The idea of not having all the answers scared me. Then it was suggested that I share with my class my apprehensiveness and fears about teaching Shakespeare. I was afraid my students would look down on me and lose respect if I admitted my weaknesses.

I was surprised to find just the opposite. By allowing myself to be a student, it allowed other students to emerge. One student who had been a problem all year began taking the class seriously and getting involved. I found myself asking him what he thought certain passages meant. We all looked forward to class. Students began reading ahead, myself included, excitedly speculating about what was going to happen next.

Letting go of my ego not only allowed some students the opportunity to lead, but also allowed me to ask for help from other teachers and to be a role model to my students. Since then, I have always chosen a book that the class and I will read together.

Sometimes a teacher helps a parent or a family to help a kid, and sometimes a teacher helps a kid to help a parent or a family.

Five qualities distinguish Unifying teachers:

1. Being a living model of growth. Unique potential and character are primarily taught by example. Hyde teachers expect a great deal from students, parents, and colleagues; therefore, they expect the same of themselves. They want students to learn organization and leadership; therefore, their own teaching reflects organized leadership. They want stu-

dents to readily admit mistakes; teachers acknowledge their own. They want students to actively seek the help of others; they themselves actively seek help. They want students to seek new challenges; they seek new challenges for themselves. The words and deeds of Hyde teachers are consistent, as are their professional and private lives.

2. Maintaining high expectations. High expectations ensure the full development of one's unique potential. Unifying teachers above all seek to inspire students. The goal is to guide students to discover and gain confidence in their unique potential. Since students must learn to value best effort over performance, the bar is set higher than what they think they can accomplish.

3. Instituting rigorous standards of discipline. Self-discipline is a cardinal skill in the discovery and development of unique potential. High expectations must be built on discipline; that which excites us without teaching us discipline is chaos. The Unifying teacher is a stickler who seldom lets go of standards of discipline. He or she assesses what the level of school discipline is and then demonstrates his or her leadership in support of it. The entire School Community is the Unifying teacher's domain.

4. Always being student-centered. The development of our own unique potential is our ultimate teacher and sensitizes us to deeper development in students. A deep reverence for unique potential strongly focuses the Hyde teacher on the student. Subjects, activities, and procedures are vehicles to draw out the deeper intellectual, emotional, and spiritual resources of students. The Unifying teacher learns to listen to students at a deep level. He or she grabs every opportunity to involve students in the learning process, constantly testing how much responsibility the students can take. The

Unifying teacher continually seeks to value student input and advice.

5. Teaching to parents and family. The unique potential journey is rooted in each student's family upbringing. The Unifying teacher fully understands that in character development, parents are the primary teachers and home the primary classroom. He or she recognizes that addressing student habits, attitudes, and deeper emotional dispositions is a fundamental part of character development, and that the deepest of these are rooted in family issues and dynamics. The Unifying teacher's dedication to the growth of students includes a dedication to the growth of parents and families.

Here Unifying teacher Paul Hurd helps two parents take hold of their responsibilities for their child's future:

> Mr. and Mrs. B sat down quietly in my office as their fifteen-year-old daughter, Bee, collapsed in a chair near them, letting out a long, heavy sigh. Summer school had just finished and Bee had completed the entire six-week program. It had been an emotional roller coaster; but unlike every other undertaking in her brief adolescence, Bee had finished it. In the school's performing arts show the night before, there was a genuine smile of pleasure and accomplishment on her face. This summer school experience had clearly been significant for her. However, the last person prepared to admit it was Bee.
>
> Mr. B opened the conversation tentatively: "I greatly appreciate what the summer has done for Bee. We see a great deal of change." He nodded in her direction. Bee was staring an intensive hole through the floor, in her attempt to avoid eye contact.
>
> Mrs. B was more assertive: "We believe she is now prepared to return and be successful at her old school." Beginning with an understatement, I queried, "What do you believe has been

the difference for her here?" Mrs. B glowed as she stated, "You asked a great deal from Bee and she responded beautifully!"

"Actually," I deadpanned, "we asked the very minimum of her and her responses varied a great deal. I think the difference in the summer was that our responses to her actions were very consistent. I don't doubt you are seeing improvement, some of which did come from Bee's effort. However, most of it came from her going through the motions of this program, and learning that when she goes off-track, we hold her accountable. I think your proposal of her return to her old school begs the question—How do you plan to hold her accountable as we have?"

Mr. B was at a total loss and Mrs. B totally miffed at these last words. Bee was completely attentive. She blurted out, "There's no way I'm coming back to this place!"

I said, "I think, Bee, you are pretty convinced you can have your own way with your parents." She replied, "So what?! You won't have anything to do with it."

I went through a litany of questions for the parents: "Is your decision based upon what you're seeing," gesturing at Bee, "or what you want to see? Are you trying to keep peace at home or challenging your daughter to grow up? Are you trying to control her or are you being controlled by her? Are you worried about the present or her future?"

Bee got up and stormed out of the room.

I simply looked at the parents and asked, "Do you believe from past experience that she feels she can manipulate you?"

"That seems quite possible," Mr. B allowed, "but we only want the best for her."

"Does she now have the perspective to clearly see her own needs?" I asked.

"Not yet," Mrs. B said.

"I'm not sure you do either," I asserted. "Look how she feels she can act around you. She learned early this summer, there's *no way we would tolerate the behavior and attitude you just saw. I implore you to consider that, to date, you three have not found the winning formula on your own."*

Mr. B said, "My wife and I need a few minutes to talk."

Three years later at Bee's graduation, all three remembered this rather unpleasant encounter with humor and gratitude.

In the Unifying process, the bar is set higher for students than what they think they can accomplish.

NOTE

1. Frank Voehl, *Deming: The Way We Knew Him* (Boca Raton, FL: CRC Press, 1995).

Part II

Tools: How to Practice
the Unifying Process

5

HEAD, HEART, SOUL

The Hierarchy in Unifying Learning

Traditional education measures progress by the achievement of goals, trying to help the student reach acceptable levels of accomplishment before moving on. The Unifying process measures progress by *individual growth*, constantly seeking to empower the student to reach the ancient Greek educational ideals: "Know thyself" and "Become what you are."

The Hyde goals might be seen as three-fold:

- Self-understanding: to realize our deeper selves and our unique potential
- Self-discipline: to distinguish and rigorously pursue our long-term *needs* rather than our short-term *wants*
- Self-confidence: to understand and trust our conscience to lead us to our destiny

So the Unifying process reflects a higher level of learning. While traditional education focuses on imparting knowledge to the student, Unifying education more comprehensibly seeks to draw out

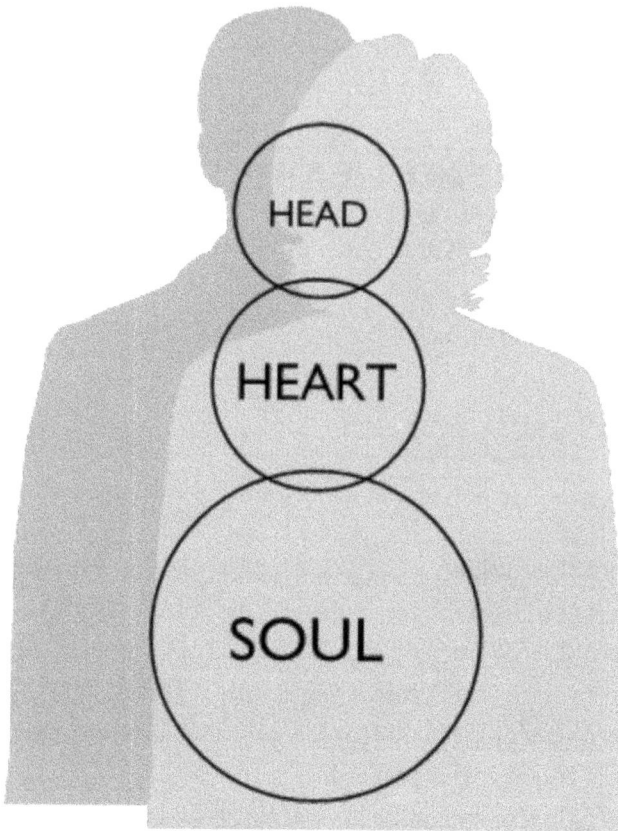

The Hierarchy in Unifying Learning. *Hyde School*

the deeper self and unique potential of the student. The difference is like drilling students on arithmetic as opposed to teaching them calculus, as the following learning stages indicate:

1. Subject-centered learning: At this most primitive level, little thought is given to what is actually happening to the student or to the student's overall growth; the only emphasis is what the student can produce in terms of a specific measurement of the acquisition of subject material.

2. Teacher-centered learning: This higher level introduces the larger efforts of the more dedicated teacher who is concerned not only with teaching the subject, but also with developing the deeper potentials in the student and preparing the student for life. This level is practiced by only some teachers, and it is usually a "hidden curriculum," one that is understood by the teacher, not necessarily by the student. The student might say twenty years later, "I'm grateful Mrs. X did what she did, and now I understand why she did it."

3. Student-centered learning: This level begins a major transformation in the learning continuum. The school community becomes primarily and openly concerned about *drawing out* the deeper potentials of students to help them prepare for meaningful lives. Since this level must emphasize the development of character, parents and the family should now increasingly become an integral part of the learning process. The teacher becomes more of a mentor to the student, and—in the Unifying process's more advanced educational setting—to parents and family as well. But even though the student is now thinking and acting more independently, the teacher is still leading. In essence, the faculty seeks to construct a "scaffolding" around the student to guide his or her learning process. The scaffolding is the Unifying culture of teachers together with the student's peers and parents, all committed to the development of the student's best and unique potential.

4. Conscience-centered learning: In classes and activities, there is a continual effort to increase the student's responsibility and accountability for the success of learning. During the spring of the senior year, the basic responsibility for learning rests primarily with the student, supported by the faculty.

The emerging senior learns to appreciate the value of learning from one's mistakes, of "choosing well" over just the freedom of choice, and of actively seeking the help of others. Ultimately the senior must realize the deeper direction of his or her conscience, and distinguish it from the lesser impulses of ego. This learning stage measures the true success of the entire program and the school itself.

So while traditional education deals just with the first two stages, Hyde deals with the two more advanced levels, which focus on the inner development of students. Teachers who have been immersed in subject-centered curricula will need help in developing these higher teaching perspectives and skills.

Obviously, since we are all creatures of habit, this is a difficult transformation for anyone schooled in traditional education. The Unifying Five Lessons, which we will discuss later in this chapter, have proven to help new students cross the bridge from their achievement orientation into our new emphasis on their unique potential and character. But first let us look at the three levels of understanding—intellectual (head), emotional (heart), and spiritual (soul)—that inform potential and mold character.

Head stands for our intellectual or thinking level of understanding. While it communicates well, it is normally our most superficial level because it is so easily controlled by our ego. (Think of the times you allowed your ego to outvote your better judgment.)

We should take care not to make the intellect our god; it has, of course, powerful muscles, but no personality. —Albert Einstein

Heart stands for our emotional and feeling level of understanding. This deeper level easily controls our egos and thus us as well. (Think of the times emotions like anger or fear blew your cool.)

It is hard to get your head and heart together in this world; in my case they are not even on speaking terms. —Woody Allen

Soul stands for our spiritual level of understanding—like conscience. We need to develop the ability to express and move beyond the power of our emotions to reach this deepest level within ourselves. (Think of how conscience can move you beyond emotions like anger or fear to help you act more maturely or courageously.)

Whatever satisfies the soul is truth. —Walt Whitman

A primary focus on the mind, even carefully constructed, still encourages the control of our egos and their excesses. A carefully constructed focus on the heart goes much deeper into ourselves and can lead to encouraging our soul potentials, like insight, intuition, imagination, and particularly conscience—the compass of our destiny—while creatively using the mind for reflection.

Every action or reaction we experience in life triggers thoughts and feelings, which in turn determine how we see ourselves and life itself. In the head-heart-soul hierarchy of learning, our feelings represent a deeper emotional level of understanding than our minds, so we are not always intellectually aware of what our feelings are or why we have them.

There are times when our minds understand something first, like a set of instructions, which we then put into practice in order to train our emotions and ourselves. For example, our minds initially try to shakily ride a bicycle, and then eventually our bodies and emotions learn to do it—flawlessly.

But more often than not, our emotions and feelings beat our minds and our thoughts to the punch. For example, how we perceive people is often heavily dependent on our first impressions of how we feel about them, and then it may take a lot to change our minds. As Blaise Pascal noted, "The heart has its reasons of which reason knows nothing."

An action-reflection cycle of learning helps us develop an identity, based on how we see ourselves and life itself (more on this in chapter 6). This identity then influences our new actions and reactions, which again trigger new thoughts and feelings. Some may reaffirm old ones, and thus lead us to conclusions that begin to form habits, attitudes, and emotional dispositions (to be addressed later in this chapter).

Our Unifying focus on character development concerns our entire self and includes not just our intellectual tools, but our emotional and spiritual tools as well. The deeper we address our actions and human potentials, the more we will realize this head-heart-soul hierarchy of understanding.

Just as we challenge ourselves to overcome the control we have over the direction of our lives, so we also challenge our deepest emotions in order to hear and be led by our conscience. As Carl Jung observed, "A man who has not passed through the inferno of his passions has never overcome them."

SOUL: OUR UNCONSCIOUS SELF

Sigmund Freud believed that in making complex decisions, we do our absolute best by relying upon such things as our insight, intuition, and ultimately our conscience.[1]

Our educational system is virtually oblivious to this vital human intelligence. Scott Kaufman's book *Ungifted: Intelligence Redefined* gives us a new definition of intelligence that factors in our deepest dreams and desires, putting the emphasis on our unconscious self, developed through such tools as insight, intuition, and conscience.

Daydreaming can be a primary means to keep this inward focus. To be effective, I believe it needs practice that must begin in childhood with the power of imagination.

Our parents control our lives, but we control our imagination. It becomes part of our world as a child. Our sense of integrity and self-confidence may ultimately depend on how we handle our developing perceptions and ideas.

I was an addictive daydreamer as a kid and my imagination made me very gullible. I remember a day at the beach when my brother and sister set up a ruse with friends to dig for buried treasure, with me as the target.

The whole time, I knew it was a joke on me, until we finally found a map that located the treasure out in the ocean. Then everyone except me gave up the game, and the next morning at breakfast, I explained to the family how we could hire a steam shovel, build a wall, and pay for it with the treasure!

Needless to say, people seldom took me seriously as a kid. I had more imagination—and less focus on life itself—which put me out of step with school and my stepfather's extensive discipline. (Now I'm thankful for his discipline and the relentless questioning that led me to finally understand math and to learn I could actually think.)

So today, with all due respect to my education, it is my unconscious—as expressed in my instincts, my intuition, and my conscience—that is central to my intelligence, not my intellect. For example, if I have a tough decision to make, I want to sleep on it to see how I view it in the morning after my unconscious has had an opportunity to digest it.

My unconscious supports my working relationships. In counseling parents, for example, I find it enables me to transcend adult protocols to help people not only in parenting, but as spouses and as individuals. As a professional, I find that conventional wisdom often blocks the deeper wisdom of parents and adults in general. We are all born with a spirit. Our imagination is crucial to expressing that spirit, and daydreaming fuels our imagination. We need parents to prepare us to deal with reality, but also to encourage our imagination.

Finally, it is up to us to ensure our imagination becomes an integral part of our own reality. If we do, we will be surprised by the power of our insight, intuition, and ultimately our conscience.

Let me demonstrate the head-heart-soul levels of understanding at work by using my own experience of climbing an eighty-foot cliff at Hurricane Island in order to confront my fear of heights.

Head: At several points on the climb, my mind told me I couldn't do it, but my ego didn't want to be humiliated by quitting in front of my son and the guide, so I kept trying, but without real conviction.

Heart: At the most dangerous point, my fear of heights took over, which illustrates my heart outvoting my ego. I was stopped cold by my fear (I had no safety rope on), and the desire not to be humiliated could no longer move me. Now I was totally expressing my deeper emotion: fear.

Soul: This confrontation with my fear finally opened me to my deepest spiritual understanding: conscience. I realized that faking an injury or quitting would leave my son with lifelong doubts about his father. My conscience reminded me that my fear was making my judgment irrational, and that I needed to trust my guide's more rational judgment; the guide was sure I could do it.

This story also demonstrates the power of synergy—my guide and my son helping me do something I couldn't do alone. So my *soul* (conscience) proved to be stronger than my *heart* (fear) at this powerful moment of truth in my life.

The Eighty-Foot Cliff at Hurricane Island. *Upward Bound USA*

It is also worth noting that it was my deeper teaching instincts that led me to the cliff experience in the first place. I knew I had to confront my fear of heights if I wanted to continue being the headmaster of a school dedicated to the development of character. Why? Because I had learned at Hyde that character must be taught by example. This realization further led me to challenge the fear that scared me most.

Two Students Lead a School Meeting. *Hyde School*

Without this deeper leadership of conscience, my ego would surely have found a rationalization to allow me to ignore (or avoid) this challenging but crucial experience.

Clearly my fear of heights can make me act irrationally, confirming that the *heart* is stronger than the *head*. However, my conscience led me to confront the fear, making the *soul* level the most powerful.

Today I still have a fear of heights, but I no longer have a fear of facing that emotion. So the entire experience has given me an even greater confidence in following my conscience, the compass of my destiny.

EMOTION IN THE UNIFYING PROCESS

My cliff example illustrates the incredible power our emotions can have over us. To effectively develop our character and unique potential, we cannot allow our emotions to control our actions. We must develop the courage to challenge ourselves at a deeper emotional level—to address feelings of fear, anxiety, frustration, anger, grief, sadness, depression, insecurity, complacency, compassion, truth, and so on. By doing so, we empower ourselves to become open to our deepest soul level of understanding, which will guide us to our destiny.

The Unifying process will challenge our deeper emotions, and the Unifying seminar (to be discussed) in particular offers us an opportunity to do it for ourselves. Dr. Christiane Northrup writes this about what she calls emotional cleansing:

> Healing can occur in the present only when we allow ourselves to feel, express, and release emotions from the past that we have suppressed or tried to forget. I call this emotional incision and drainage. I've often likened this deeper process to the treatment of an abscess. Any surgeon knows that the treatment of an abscess is to cut it open, allowing the pus to drain. When this is done, the pain goes away almost immediately, and new tissue can reform where the abscess once was. It is the same with emotions. They too become walled off, causing pain and absorbing energy, if we do not release them.[2]

Some in the psychiatric community once questioned the value of addressing past and painful traumas. Doing so in some cases, they warned, may simply add more pain; "suppressing" them may actually be better medicine. We would say that as long as our goal is the realization of our unique potential and destiny, addressing any emotional roadblock would ultimately be necessary and positive.

We can empower ourselves to become open to our deepest soul level of understanding, which will guide us to our destiny.

Identifying and expressing our deeper emotions in seminar settings is particularly important in helping parents to let go of their own parents (and particular childhood experiences) in order to move on in their own lives and properly let go of their children. Students need to identify and express their deeper emotions to fully realize their character and unique potential, as do teachers in order to model this deeper growth for students and parents.

EGO AND CONSCIENCE: OUR LEARNING GUIDES

Our understanding and sensitivity to our conscience, together with our management of ego, will ultimately determine how well we fulfill our true destiny in life.

We constantly have to make decisions and experience reactions in life, so our ego acts as sort of a personal computer to rapidly sort them all out and choose how best to cope or react.

In psychoanalytic theory, ego is defined as "the organized conscious mediator between the person and reality, especially by functioning both in the perception of and adaptation to reality."

The ego reflects a compromise between how we view ourselves and how we perceive the truth. Without discipline, the ego can easily become more enamored with self than with reality—note that the term "ego trip" has earned a place in *Webster's Dictionary*.

The ego is not master in its own house. —Sigmund Freud

In truth, we have far more difficulty with deflated egos that keep us from realizing the power of our deeper potentials.

Webster's defines conscience as "the moral goodness . . . of one's own conduct, intentions, or character together with a feeling of obligation to do right or be good."

A good conscience is a continual Christmas. —Benjamin Franklin

We take this definition a vital step further by defining conscience: the inner voice that serves as the compass to one's destiny. More than just a "traffic cop" of right and wrong, conscience in our view is a central guidance system that can tell us the best path to fulfill our unique potential and destiny.

We should not think of ego as bad and conscience as good.

In fact, a big ego is essential to our creating big things. But the ego needs to be guided by conscience or it will easily get beyond its supportive role and cause us problems. Ego is the sergeant that directs us in the day-to-day trenches of life, and conscience the general that oversees the strategy and direction of our entire life.

The ego is generally tuned to our instant wants, while our conscience is tuned to our long-term needs. This is why our capacity to delay gratification is so crucial to our well-being and ultimate fulfillment.

The Unifying process perceives conscience as a profound inner wisdom primarily created by a power and a purpose beyond ourselves. It links our own larger purpose in life to the destiny of others and to universal forces. It can draw upon the conscience of others, while at the same time connecting to and drawing from our own unique heritage and potentials.

The Relationship between Ego and Conscience

If we perceive ourselves as a mass of instincts, thoughts, feelings, conditioned responses, fears and phobias, wants and needs, then our ego wades through all the information, looks at reality, and comes up with a conclusion that is a reasonable compromise. (Recall the definition of ego: the organized conscious mediator between the person and reality.)

But how ego mediates this compromise depends upon us. If we want something bad enough, ego will help us get it. If we fear something enough, ego will help us avoid it. If we don't like a situation enough, ego can even help us revise reality and the truth!

Without interference, this instant-gratification ego system would make us creatures of our most unproductive thoughts and feelings. It explains how our addictions and phobias come to overpower us.

Fortunately, we are also endowed with a conscience, a deeper and more comprehensive inner guidance system. The foundation for conscience is supported by our parents with right-wrong, good-bad conditioning.

During the teen years, our capacity to hear and understand our conscience needs to be challenged and formally developed. One crucial step is learning a deep reverence for the truth, essential to developing a healthy and productive ego that will be led by conscience. It is up to each of us to train our ego to respect our best and to consistently obey the dictates of our conscience.

With the Action-Reflection Learning Cycle (see chapter 6), we are less concerned with the specific reactions and behaviors of a student and more concerned with what these reactions and behaviors suggest about the student's ego and sense of identity. When the student's ego and identity are developing well, so are his or her reactions and behaviors.

ADDRESSING WHATEVER INTERFERES WITH THE UNIFYING GROWTH PROCESS

We must carefully monitor our human development to achieve our best growth. We are imperfect, and our lesser self-protection and self-gratification instincts sometimes lead us into wrong actions that become counterproductive habits. By putting counterproductive habits and attitudes into action, we develop counterproductive emotional dispositions. And once we put counterproductive emotional dispositions into action, we can easily begin to follow paths that compromise the path of our character and true destiny, and make us less than what we truly are.

For example, given the high expectations we develop for ourselves, we may begin to view our actions in life as indicating that we lack the capability to fulfill our expectations, thus developing a counterproductive lack of confidence that restricts our performance.

It is vital to understand that all of us, through no fault of our own, have negative emotional dispositions (NEDs) from childhood that we need to address if we hope to realize our best in life, a requirement to fully discovering our unique potential and destiny.

We have imitated our parents from birth. So we are empowered by the struggles that revealed their character, values, and sense of purpose; but at the same time, we carry the burden of their inevitable imperfections. The more our parents—or their ancestors—strived to accomplish in life, the more problems and imperfections they inevitably developed. We imitated those imperfections (NEDs) as well.

But if parents and children can simply accept that we have NEDs (imitated in childhood) that we need to address, our growth will become much steadier and stronger.

What are these NEDs we develop in childhood? Let me give you my personal examples.

My stepfather's integrity, self-discipline, and sense of purpose (positive emotional dispositions, or PEDs) have inspired my own character. But the biggest challenge in my childhood was developing the courage to transcend a deep inferiority complex and cowardice (NED) I developed, primarily in response to his deep imbalance of criticism versus encouragement. I later understood how this imbalance was rooted in his own upbringing.

I was encouraged by my mother's belief in me and I internalized her genuine concern for others (PED). But my most difficult challenge in life was dealing with a very warped sense of loyalty (NED) that I developed in response to her unresolved alcoholism—which was rooted in *her* mother's alcoholism.

It took me fifteen years to let go of this warped sense of loyalty—and of my wife Blanche's alcoholism, rooted in her own family's alcoholism. When I finally did (with the help of Al-Anon), my children let go as well. That's when Blanche finally found sobriety, and our remarriage reunited our family.

Those often painful fifteen years expressed the NED I had developed in dealing with my mother's unresolved alcoholism. My misguided sense of loyalty in standing by my mother, and then trying to help Blanche in the same way, actually enabled their drinking! Once I transcended my NED to gain a higher sense of loyalty, I finally got out of Blanche's way, and she solved her problem. I just wish I had done it sooner.

We all have similar stories to tell. Our parents inevitably developed their own PEDs and NEDs, and our own growth is significantly affected by them. Sibling dispositions can also affect us.

In acknowledgment of the destructiveness of NEDs, Dr. Robert Anda of the Centers for Disease Control and Prevention and Dr. Vincent Felitti of Kaiser Permanente conducted a major study of the adverse childhood experiences (ACEs) of seventeen thousand individuals (average age 57). They found the long-term effects of ACEs "surprisingly common." According to the study, fifty years post-childhood, these experiences "transformed from psychosocial experience into organic disease, social malfunction and mental illness."[3]

They significantly concluded that ACEs "are the main determinant of the health and social well-being of the nation."

Whatever we may achieve in life, we will owe a huge debt of gratitude to those who raised us, no matter how they may have also failed us. Isaac Newton, arguably the world's greatest contributor, said, "If I have been able to see further, it is only because I stood on the shoulders of giants." In life we stand on the shoulders of those who parented us far more than we realize.

By recognizing the values, attitudes, and character our parents and families instilled in us, along with recognizing the unresolved family issues that were passed on to us, we can better assess our growth, while still honoring their contribution. This will make us stronger individuals, teachers, and parents, while also making us more sensitive to help we need. It is nature's plan that in addition to our own efforts, we learn to rely on others to realize our true best and our unique potential.

The farther behind I leave the past, the closer I am to forging my own character. —Isabelle Eberhardt

There is nothing so easy to learn as experience and nothing so hard to apply. —Josh Billings

THE FIVE LESSONS: INTRODUCING THE UNIFYING PROCESS

Over the years we have learned a process that helps new students cross the bridge from their achievement orientation into our new emphasis on their unique potential and character. We call it the Five Lessons.

Let's imagine we are beginning with two hundred new teenagers, from all kinds of family backgrounds, who are supporting a wide range of attitudes and personas they developed in coping with today's achievement system. False bravado. Shy and retiring. "I don't care." "I don't want to be here." Clothes-conscious. No confidence. The loner. The joiner. "I'm above it all." "I can't do it." Good-time Charlie. The quitter.

Regardless of how confident or mature he or she might seem, we find that every teenager (like every adult) harbors at least some unproductive attitudes or images.

We want to help youngsters shed these defenses and become confident in just being themselves, the key to developing their true potential. So we begin by guiding them through the Five Lessons:

1. Take a risk and have fun. The first step builds on their risk-taking instincts and natural curiosity. We begin by giving them a wide range of challenges: navigating a high ropes course, completing a series of physical challenges where it takes teamwork to succeed, introducing themselves clearly to the entire school, singing a solo on stage, sharing their deeper thoughts and feelings in a group, participating in a

"trust fall" where they must place their safety in the hands of others. Our goal is to find something that challenges every student. (*Just keep taking chances and have fun.* —Garth Brooks)

2. Put best effort over performance. At this point, hopefully every student has had some fun, done some things they were both good and terrible at, and experienced a wide range of emotions—elation to fear to the agony of defeat. But as they observe these same feelings in their peers, they begin to realize that both success and failure are simply par for the course, that real winning is a matter of always putting forth one's best effort—trying hard, not quitting, persevering, maintaining a good attitude, helping others—regardless of the outcome. Hyde's top academic graduate one year devoted his entire speech (every senior speaks at graduation) to what he had learned about himself in JV wrestling! (*Continuous effort—not strength or intelligence—is the key to unlocking our potential.* —Winston Churchill)

3. Be yourself. The challenges have now "popped" some attitudes and stripped away some images. Sometimes kids have surprised themselves with what they can do. Sometimes they have acted like jerks—and were told so. Sometimes they have really tried to help others—and later found out their efforts were appreciated. Sometimes they failed themselves, and then became determined to do better. Their deeper selves become exposed, and they begin to realize they'd rather be this true inner guy, warts and all, than some of the artificial images they continually have to prop up. (*Be yourself; everyone else is already taken.* —Oscar Wilde)

4. Bet on the truth. As the students begin to take some risks, face some fears, shed some images, and become more their true selves, a deeper sense of honesty begins to emerge.

Regardless of what some people might think, adolescents are not comfortable in relationships that are not completely honest; they thrive in environments that they trust have a primary commitment to the truth, and they will work to keep it that way. In the teenage world, being called "fake" is the worst criticism. (*Truth never damages a cause that is just.* —Mahatma Gandhi)

5. Support each other's best. We all have a deeper instinct that wants to help others; it will surface in kids when they trust their peers are being themselves and are willing to bet on the truth. In this atmosphere of challenge, young people sometimes felt exposed at their worst, and yet discovered their peers genuinely tried to support them and didn't look down on them. They saw some of their peers feeling the same way, and felt compelled to help them as well. Now kids begin to move away from cliques and selective relationships, and the foundation for the Hyde Brother's/Sister's Keeper ethic begins to form. (*Life's most persistent and urgent question is: What are you doing for others?* —Martin Luther King Jr.)

The Five Lessons teach students to appreciate challenge, best effort and attitude, being open and honest, and helping each other. This work sets the stage to challenge students academically. For example, Susie, who "can't do math," knows that she faces no greater challenge than uncoordinated Tom in athletics or tone-deaf Jane in performing arts. She knows her classmates will expect her best effort. We know she will surprise herself once she really tries, and her curiosity will begin to motivate her to a higher level. With all students taking this attitude, academic excellence becomes inevitable. While Hyde-Bath seldom screens students academically, 97 percent of them have gone on to four-year colleges.

Students Experiencing a Fun Competition. *Hyde School*

IPSES: ENGAGING THE FIVE DEEPER RESOURCES OF STUDENTS

The Five Lessons teach us that the Unifying process begins with fully challenging the student. We seek to excite students about discovering their deeper potentials, not to fear their potential shortcomings, and to ultimately trust that their best efforts will ensure their fulfillment in life. We find that students have five deeper potentials or resources that must be fully addressed in this learning process. We refer to these aspects of living as IPSES: Intellectual, Physical, Social, Emotional, and Spiritual.

We seek to develop these deeper resources whenever possible, and we have elevated athletics, performing arts, community service, and jobs as much as possible to academic courses in order to emphasize this overall development in students.

1. Intellectual: Our college preparatory academic program helps to emphasize the student's intellectual development. However, to intellectually fully challenge each and every student, we stress that *attitude is valued over aptitude, effort over ability, and character over talent.* We define the term "intellectual character" as an appreciation of the student's curiosity, dedication, participation, persistence, and excellence, particularly in the classroom setting.

2. Physical: Our athletic program helps to emphasize the student's physical development. Our jobs program helps them to develop both physically and socially. And when a student has "attitude" problems, we have found that physical tasks and work can lead students to think more constructively about themselves.

3. Social: Our community action program helps students find and express their deeper concern for others, and leads some students to glimpse an important part of their unique potential. Further, the common commitment of students, teachers, and parents creates a united and powerful School Community in which members learn a dedication to help each other do their best.

4. Emotional: Our performing arts program helps students express and appreciate their deeper and more emotional selves. We also find that journaling exercises, seminars (in which we share deep feelings in groups), and school meetings are important activities to help students connect their truer thoughts and feelings.

5. Spiritual: We view spiritual resources as reflecting our deepest and innermost selves, which include the expression of our conscience. We find that as we help students fully develop their intellectual, physical, social, and emotional resources, their spiritual resources become naturally ex-

pressed in the process. The spirit of the school itself may reflect the overall spiritual development of the students. Interestingly, one family built and donated a small building with circular seating, next to the duck pond, as a place for people to meditate. The students call it "the Spiritual Center" and use it for such occasions.

All of these five resources are involved in our actions to some degree. It helps when there is a concerted effort to point out their specific development.

At different times in the year, students (as well as faculty and parents) may choose, or be asked, to assess their level of care or growth regarding each of the IPSES areas.

FIVE STAGES OF LEARNING: BUILDING BLOCKS IN THE UNIFYING PROCESS

Up to this point, we haven't considered the *readiness* of the student to learn. Clearly the motivation of the student is the crucial factor in how effective any educational process will work. So we take great care in developing the student's role in the Unifying process.

There is a five-stage learning process that students experience as they practice the Unifying process: Off-Track, Motions, Effort, Consistency, and Excellence.

While students may begin at different readiness levels, let's trace the most difficult student.

1. Off-Track: This stage requires a major adjustment in the student's learning process. The Action-Reflection Learning Cycle tells us *how* a student learns, but not *if* they will learn, or *when* they will learn. The *if* requires student motivation.

It is senseless to try to teach a student a lesson he or she is
not motivated to learn. We refer to such unmotivated students as *off-track*—perhaps describing a student motivated
in a different or wrong direction, or at least not in a charac-
ter-driven, positive direction. We prescribe a special program for off-track students, designed to help them think
more deeply about what they are doing—a vital step to begin to motivate them to participate in self-discovery and the
Unifying program.

This is a challenge to public schools, but one worth a real creative
effort to achieve. At the same time, the Unifying process will be
making inroads to deeper student involvement, so there should be
minimal resistance.

It is also senseless to try to teach students lessons they aren't
properly prepared to learn—like trying to teach a subject to students before they have mastered the basic skills involved. The
Hyde process is sensitive to what actually can be expected from a
student and then guides the student accordingly.

2. Motions: In this teacher-directed stage of learning, the student is expected only to demonstrate the "motions" of learning. He or she doesn't have to like, understand, or agree
   with it—only do it. Once the student actually begins to imitate the actions of a true student, his or her deeper self will
   begin to internalize the learning and have some success,
   which will trigger his or her curiosity.

3. Effort: Growing success leads the student to initiate some of
   the learning process, which begins a partnership role with
   the teacher. The Effort stage begins to trigger the curiosity
   and motivation of the student toward more learning.

4. Consistency: In time, the student can be primarily trusted
   with maintaining the quality of his or her work. Without

significant interruption, this stage is the natural conse-
quence of effort learning.

5. Excellence: This student-directed stage shows the student
actively pursuing his or her best, while helping others in the
process.

Traditional learning is complicated by the reality that students
generally are at different stages in both motivation and prepared-
ness to learn. One student may be well trained, another learning
disabled; one eager, another distracted; one confident, another
prone to giving up; and so forth. However, the Unifying process
addresses and builds on the unique situation and learning style of
each student. Assuming a strong family commitment, we are confident the process will ultimately nurture and work for *every* student, even though the path to get there will vary from student to
student.

EXCELLENCE
THE GIVER
- Going after one's best is paramount
- "Prime the pump:" Givers who seek to help others
- Set a standard for other students to follow
- Teachers and Parents "Let Go."

CONSISTENCY
THE ACHIEVER
- Accepts the primary responsibility for learning
- Cements the student-teacher bond
- Work ethic is trusted
- An active learner open to challenges

EFFORT
THE DOER
- Beginnings of a positive attitude
- "If I have to this, I might as well do it well"
- Student and teacher bond and begin sharing expectations
- Feelings are expressed and creativity emerges

MOTIONS
THE TAKER
- The "motions" of responsible behavior
- "Move the body and the mind will follow"
- Expectations are set by the faculty
- Sometimes an unpleasant phase
- The foundation is set for personal growth and the discovery of unique potential

FOUNDATION (repeated across grid)

Stages of Learning. *Hyde School*

So let us first discuss the student's readiness to enter the Motions-Effort-Consistency-Excellence continuum.

Family Commitment

A crucial step in applying the Unifying process can come from the commitment made by both parent/guardian/mentor and student. The school's in-depth approach to student growth is ensured by continual family support. Every student is going to be challenged to new levels they may not feel ready or willing to meet. Without some backing from home, the school could be powerless to help students over these crucial personal hurdles.

The Unifying program seeks to continually challenge the student. When parents are on board, students' refusal to comply or stubborn resistance to direction are easier to deal with. Recalcitrant attitudes can then become also the *family's* problem to solve, with the school working closely with the parents. Thus, we seek to gain a strong home commitment, and a particularly strong one from the student if the parental commitment seems to be shaky. We want the Unifying process for all our students, so we recognize the powerful role the family plays in our success.

A Hyde staffer visiting a fifty-five-student classroom in China was shocked that the teacher ignored a student who was sleeping, and asked why. He was calmly told discipline was the parents' job and the school would report the student's behavior to them; the school's job was educating students. Obviously, a good dose of that attitude would significantly help American schools.

Schools that seek to adopt the Unifying process should make a strong effort to contact the parents of their students. Beyond sending descriptions of the program to them, it would be wise to hold a meeting at the school so they could hear about it and ask questions. They should also have an opportunity to get to know the

Discovery Group leaders who will be their children's guides. Hyde charter schools even arrange parent-student retreats.

Since the home is the primary student influence, it is vital to first determine the extent to which a student's unsatisfactory performance at school reflects family issues and attitudes versus just those of the individual student. If the family commitment of a recalcitrant student can be confirmed, the student can be confidently placed in the Off-Track learning stage.

AN IN-DEPTH LOOK AT THE FIVE STAGES OF LEARNING

When a student's progress or behavior is deemed poor or unacceptable, the student is usually considered to be off-track. This means the student needs a more specialized learning approach before he or she is ready to resume the normal Unifying student routine. We find it counterproductive to try to move students ahead when their motivation, attitudes, and readiness need to be addressed.

Dealing with the off-track student is usually a matter of degree. At Hyde-Bath, it might involve:

- A conference with a teacher or administrator
- A "concern meeting" with students and teachers
- An afternoon or early morning work program
- A Saturday family conference and work session

If all this fails, we come up with something innovative that works—usually a program that no one would choose to employ. But doing this conveys to the off-track student how committed we are.

Once the family commitment has been confirmed and any off-track attitudes and behavior have been successfully addressed, students are then ready to enter the other four stages: Motions, Effort, Consistency, Excellence. These represent a growth process that leads to the discovery and fulfillment of unique potential.

Imagine we want to teach an intricate dance step to a group of teenagers whose views of this exercise range from "I can't do it" to "This is stupid." As long as we can get them to disregard their off-track attitudes and at least go through the motions of the steps, we ultimately will be successful with them. They don't have to like it, understand it, or even *think* they can do it; they only have to do it, because in time, their bodies will come to understand, and their own inner guidance system will eventually begin to lead them.

Once their bodies actually begin to internalize the step—which "motions" practice makes inevitable—the youngsters may then become curious about their capabilities and at least say to themselves, "Well, if I *have* to do it, I may as well do it well."

Now they enter the Effort stage, where they themselves are providing some of the motivation that was earlier just the teacher's. If they stick with it, they will ultimately enter the Consistency stage, where their own interest and effort allows us to trust the standards they are setting for themselves. From there, they can enter the Excellence stage, where they have internalized the steps well enough to begin their own innovations that will take them beyond what we initially taught them.

This roughly describes how we develop unique potential in youngsters. We begin with a dedicated commitment of a teacher students have come to trust enough to at least go through the motions. In time these motions will inevitably interest, even inspire, the student to begin to put effort into developing his or her own unique potential.

Why does this occur? Because each youngster in fact *is* gifted with a unique potential that defines a destiny, which requires only faith to put in motion! And this faith leads to further unique potential development that inspires an even deeper faith, an endless cycle that, left unbroken, will ultimately lead the youngster into the Excellence stage.

This amazing faith/unique potential cycle initiated by the teacher explains why the most often heard phrase at a Hyde graduation is "You believed in me when I didn't believe in myself." This comment is directed to the graduating senior's parents and teachers.

NOTES

1. Saul McLeod, "Freud and the Unconscious Mind," SimplyPsychology, 2015, https://www.simplypsychology.org/unconscious-mind.html.

2. Christiane Northrup, *Women's Bodies, Women's Wisdom: Creating Physical and Emotional Health and Healing* (New York: Bantam, 2010).

3. Vincent J. Felitti, "The Origins of Addiction: Evidence from the Adverse Childhood Experiences Study," Kaiser Permanente, February 16, 2004, https://www.nijc.org/pdfs/Subject%20Matter%20Articles/Drugs%20and%20Alc/ACE%20Study%20-%20OriginsofAddiction.pdf.

6

THE ACTION-REFLECTION LEARNING CYCLE

Nature often provides us a process for doing things. Take golf. Many golfers try to overpower the ball in an ego attempt to hit it long, and end up frustrated as it curves out of bounds. What they don't realize is that centrifugal force is what really powers a golf ball and the professional golfer develops a powerful rhythmic swing in support of it to hit the ball long and under control.

This ancient proverb well describes the Unifying process:

> Sow a thought, reap an act;
> sow an act, reap a habit;
> sow a habit, reap a character;
> sow a character, reap a destiny.

And here is how it works: By repeatedly using the Action-Reflection Learning Cycle, we begin to transform right ideas into actions, then right actions into habits. By repeatedly practicing right habits, we begin to develop our true character. By putting our true character into action—living by our principles—we are led on the path of our true destiny.

Hyde Student Shares a Moment Following a Soccer Game. *Hyde School*

Traditional education largely ignores this deeper growth process, entrusting it to family and chance. The Unifying process embraces the family and community, forming a character-based culture in order to systematically draw out the unique potential of each individual.

Individuals artistically express their words and actions at an even deeper spiritual level, like in music or, perhaps, a great athletic performance.

This character-based culture creates a strong "cocoon."

Breaking out of our family cocoon is meant to be one of the most difficult challenges we face in life. Consider this observation of how nature's cocoon works:

"The Butterfly"

One day a man found a cocoon of a butterfly. When a small opening appeared, he sat and watched the butterfly for several hours through the tiny hole.

Then it seemed to stop making progress. It had gotten as far as it could, and could go no farther.

So the man decided to help the butterfly. He took a pair of scissors and snipped off the remaining bit of the cocoon. The butterfly now emerged easily. But it had a swollen body and small, shriveled wings.

The man continued to watch the butterfly because he expected that, at any moment, the wings would enlarge and expand, to be able to support the body, which would contract in time.

Neither happened. In fact, the butterfly spent the rest of its life crawling around with a swollen body and shriveled wings. It never was able to fly.

What the man, in his kindness and haste, did not understand was that the restricting cocoon, and the struggle required for the butterfly to get through the tiny opening, were nature's way of forcing fluid from the body of the butterfly into its wings so that it would be ready for flight once it achieved freedom from the cocoon.

Sometimes struggles are exactly what we need in our life. If we were allowed to go through life without any obstacles, it would cripple us.

We would not be as strong as we could have been. And we would never be able to fly.

Just as nature's cocoon transforms the caterpillar into a butterfly, so must we transform into a higher human self.

Caterpillar Transforming into a Butterfly. *Hyde School*

Nature does nothing uselessly. —Aristotle

The powerful lesson of nature's cocoon is this: we humans are meant to struggle in life; this may be why we are continually exposed to such striking opposites as pain and joy, good and evil, and so on. We must teach this truth to our children, not with words, but by helping them experience it.

So just as exiting nature's cocoon becomes the major life challenge to the caterpillar, so should breaking out of the Unifying cocoon serve as a challenge to the growing adolescent. The caterpillar must force its bodily fluids into its wings in order to break out of nature's cocoon, which in turn enables it to fly. Adolescents must be required to rely on their deeper intellectual, physical, social, emotional, and spiritual resources in order to begin to realize their unique potential and destiny.

Then, just as the professional golfer utilizes centrifugal force to create a beautiful and powerful swing, so does the adolescent begin to utilize character and unique potential to follow a path to a meaningful and fulfilling life.

TRADITIONAL EDUCATION VS. THE UNIFYING PROCESS

We should understand the tremendous difference between academic learning—the way we were all taught in school—and character growth, the way we learn in a Unifying school. It is like comparing one-dimensional learning to three-dimensional learning.

In traditional education, we learn a lesson with just our mind and then move on, even if we later forget it. In character development we utilize our mind, heart, body, and soul, and then continually repeat our lessons in order to internalize them.

Picture the static traditional classroom where most of the action simply occurs between the minds of teacher and student. To picture a classroom in a character-based culture, imagine a dramatic play where the players must first learn to integrate both their lines and actions, then continually work to internalize them so they can be expressed at a deeper emotional level. Finally, in

great performances, individuals artistically express their words and
actions at an even deeper level, like in music or perhaps an athletic
performance. ("He's in the zone!")

So the Unifying process might be seen as occurring in these
steps:

1. Learn and integrate our thoughts and actions.
2. Work to more deeply internalize our thoughts and actions.
3. Learn to express our thoughts and actions at intellectual,
   emotional, and spiritual levels.
4. Address whatever interferes with this character growth process.

What follows gives a more detailed look at each of these steps.

LEARNING AND INTEGRATING OUR THOUGHTS AND ACTIONS

The acquisition of knowledge in traditional schooling inevitably
puts the focus on the teacher and the teacher's mind. Our new
emphasis on character shifts the educational focus to the student
and the student's growth, which in turn puts the premium on the
student's actions. A Chinese proverb wisely notes: "I hear—and I
forget; I see—and I remember; I do—and I understand."

Therefore, our Unifying emphasis is on *challenge*, because
challenge begins the process of drawing out the deeper resources
of the student.

Instead of the traditional approach of giving students the lessons and then expecting them to show their mastery in written or
oral words, the Hyde process utilizes challenges to initiate lessons.

As the students experience these challenges, they learn to reflect upon their own responses to them, which further form their

sense of identity. We then expect students to demonstrate by their actions and character that they are mastering the lessons the challenges initiated.

Off-track teenagers are naturally challenged by having to struggle with their poor decisions, behavior, attitudes, addictions, and so on in order to put their lives together. But how do we challenge the more "perfect" students who seem to handle traditional academic, athletic, behavioral, and other responsibilities with ease? Ken Grant was the first "perfect" Hyde student and it finally became my responsibility to provide the challenge and struggle he needed to truly discover himself.

Ken writes:

Perhaps the most meaningful experience in my life came one October morning when I walked into Mr. Gauld's office to ask for a recommendation for college. . . . I distinctly remember his looking deeply into my eyes and saying, "Ken, you need a challenge and a struggle. I want you to go out and do something against your creeds and your values, then come back and let me know how you feel." This statement was forceful and direct; Mr. Gauld left no option.

I left his office totally perplexed and scared. I remember as I walked down the hall how my eyes got misty. I do recall telling my parents, I guess looking for comfort and support. I didn't get it. They were both perplexed, but my mother's only reply was, "Well, what are you going to do?"

I struggled within, only telling one or two of my closest friends about the talk. A week passed and I still hadn't done anything; my conscience wouldn't let me. Finally, I just had to talk with Mr. Gauld. I was really scared, probably visibly so. After all, I was defying his authority.

I simply said, "Mr. Gauld, I can't do what you ask; my conscience won't let me." I was ready for lightening to strike. Yet the only response from Mr. Gauld was a huge smile, full of

warmth and love. To say the least, I was totally perplexed. I
just couldn't grasp the meaning of our encounter.

In college, the meaning became clearer to Ken:

I found college a struggle. In my first two years, I spent little
time reflecting on what I was doing. Then by my junior and
senior years, I began to realize something . . . I was intimidated
by college.

I was doing what was expected of me, not to please just
myself, but my professors and coaches. I would give 100 per-
cent of myself, but only get 20 percent in return.

I began to question their attitudes, accountability, and au-
thority. I became actively involved in student groups, strug-
gling to make someone accountable for our education. In short,
college and authority no longer intimidated me.

This experience finally explained my encounter with Mr.
Gauld. He knew that Hyde's ethical codes were basic to my life.
Yet he also knew that authority intimidated me. So he chal-
lenged me to stand on my own two feet and demand respect for
my being. I now understand Mr. Gauld's smile and realize the
strength within me.

Ken later became part of the Hyde leadership team and served as
the founding headmaster of one of our Hyde Schools.

We call this learning process the *Action-Reflection Learning
Cycle.*

In public schools utilizing the Hyde process, students participate in weekly Discovery Groups of twelve to fifteen mixed-grade
students under the direction of the homeroom teacher. The group
shares an active program involving athletics, performing arts, community service, and jobs (taking care of the school community).
They often "seminar," continually reviewing their actions, attitudes, thoughts, and feelings and sharing with the group. Group

members respond with feedback to what each student shared, offering observations, support, and sometimes challenges to the student.

For example, a student struggling with self-confidence might share that fact with the group, which in itself is an important step in developing a deeper sense of identity. Then, in gaining the responses and insights of others, a new plan of action—or step to take to move forward—could be developed, and then put into practice.

Given the student's effort and dedication to growth, the follow-up in future Discovery Group meetings (as well as in conversations with group members outside of the specific Discovery Group time) would almost ensure that the student's growth will help him or her gain a more positive sense of confidence and identity.

INTERNALIZING OUR THOUGHTS AND ACTIONS

The Action-Reflection Learning Cycle begins with a wide set of challenges undertaken by every student, teacher, and parent. (Remember, character is learned primarily by example.) Challenges are put forth in all areas of school life: academics, athletics, performing arts, community service, speaking to the school, singing a solo on stage, teaching others, jobs and leadership roles, and retreat or wilderness experiences. Vacations and home life are also an integral part of this personal learning process. Hyde families are taught to operate as a Discovery Group unit for all family members.

Next comes the reflection part of the cycle, where we think about our actions and behaviors in response to these challenges. Reflections may take place in journals written by students, in discussions in Discovery Groups, in school seminars, in concern meetings called to discuss the growth of a single individual or family, in school meetings, in one-on-one conferences, in senior evaluations, and in family seminars. Students get into the habit of conducting deep, Discovery Group–level discussions in their Unifying relationships and sometimes even with friends at home. The point is to try to tie every action to a reflection, where we think about what we are doing and who we are. These reflections lead to new perceptions of our attitudes and ourselves; these new perceptions are then tested by simply repeating the learning cycle.

We don't see things as they are, we see them as we are.

—Anaïs Nin

In this way we become far more aware of how others see our actions, habits, and attitudes, helping us reaffirm positive ones and motivating us to change unproductive ones.

Rigorous academic training is an integral part of this learning process; we have found that students become more deeply motivated academically because it is essential to their self-discovery.

Character emphasis makes a Unifying School a very active and very reflective place. Students are challenged with as much responsibility as they can handle in terms of both the school and their own growth.

In addition, the three basic questions—*Who am I? Where am I going? What do I need to get there?*—require a great deal of reflection, particularly in seminar settings, for students and faculty to benefit from the Unifying program's most powerful tool: synergy.

The Action-Reflection Learning Cycle drives the Unifying program. It begins with a wide set of challenges and continues with a wide range of opportunities: one-on-one conversations, Discovery

Groups, school meetings, concern meetings, and particularly seminars.

UNIFYING SEMINARS: ARTICULATING OUR THOUGHTS AND ACTIONS TO ENABLE CHARACTER GROWTH

A Unifying seminar is defined as any gathering—primarily involving students, teachers, and parents—devoted to sharing issues of personal and character growth. The group could be five to twenty people—or even larger. The success of a seminar is connected to the depth of sharing.

The seminar reflects what the early Greeks taught us to seek: our unique potential that yearns to be expressed and lived. By transcending our lesser feelings and emotions, we open ourselves to the deeper and more powerful intellectual, emotional, and spiritual resources of our higher human self and our unique destiny.

Many of the habits, attitudes, and emotional dispositions we develop will move our growth along the path of our unique destiny. It is important to recognize and reinforce positive ones, and understand that others may retard, block, or misdirect our growth. Since the habits, attitudes, and emotional dispositions we form are very difficult to change, and particularly so by ourselves alone, the synergy of the Unifying seminar is a powerful way not only to effectively deal with them, but also to transcend those that do not support our growth.

Our unique destiny requires our true best, and we realize that we cannot achieve our true best alone. We have learned that others see our best and our unique potential in ways we ourselves cannot.

THE ACTION - REFLECTION CYCLE FOR GROWTH

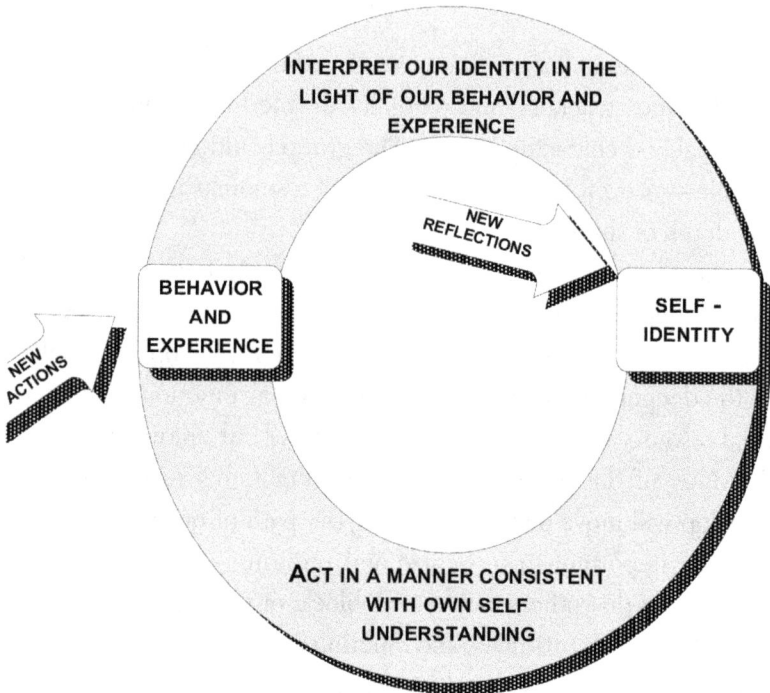

INTERPRET OUR IDENTITY IN THE
LIGHT OF OUR BEHAVIOR AND
EXPERIENCE

NEW
REFLECTIONS

BEHAVIOR
AND
EXPERIENCE

SELF -
IDENTITY

NEW
ACTIONS

ACT IN A MANNER CONSISTENT
WITH OWN SELF
UNDERSTANDING

The Action-Reflection Cycle for Growth. *Hyde School*

When we try to apply the Action-Reflection Learning Cycle by ourselves, our emotions or our egos can easily overwhelm our thoughts or block our conscience. But when we apply this learning cycle in seminar settings, others help us to move beyond our emotions and egos to reach our true best.

Learning to Experience and Utilize Seminar Synergy

Three important seminar thoughts will help us maximize the power of synergy in our growth:

1. Primarily share from our actual experiences in life, and try to share them like an objective reporter. Editing the experience to what we think is significant and important may short-circuit the deeper insights of others. Learn to share experiences as they are; then if we feel the need, add more. Remember, others can always ask if they don't understand something.
2. Share as deeply as we can from our feelings and our emotions, not from our thoughts and our mind. The goal in a seminar is always to learn how to understand and then follow conscience—the compass of our destiny. What we share from our feelings and our emotions puts us just one step away from conscience, while what we share from our minds and our thoughts is always controlled by us and our egos— two steps away from conscience.
3. Listen with an open mind and heart; encourage and allow others to share their deeper thoughts and feelings in seminars. In this way we achieve their maximum contribution to our best. A key seminar guideline is if the shoe fits, wear it; if not, throw it away. Remember we and we alone will decide what we will take away from seminars, so we should encourage others to be honest with us.

Emotional growth is critical in character development. For our emotions such as hate, anger, frustration, guilt, shame, sorrow, and humiliation, the acid test is: Are they changing us for the better or not? If they are, continue to hold on to them. If not, get rid of them or transcend them, which we can do by beginning to share them in seminars.

Think of the irrational fears that our self-protection instincts can produce. Think of the irrational desires that our self-gratification instincts can create. Think of how our inherent self-centeredness can center the world on our wants and ourselves. The synergy we can experience in seminars puts into motion the power we need to transcend these lesser-self qualities.

So in approaching seminar homework and participation, we take a deeper look at ourselves and our growth:

- We review our experiences, past and present. We share positive experiences that we want to acknowledge to ourselves and have reinforced by others. We share and acknowledge negative ones and allow the input of others to help us move beyond them. No one is perfect, and we should never allow our mistakes and shortcomings to diminish us or stand in our way.

- We review our feelings and emotions in response to life, particularly those that intellectually we do not fully understand. It takes courage to go to this deeper emotional level because we give up control and may experience confusion and uncertainty. But seminars may lead us to a deeper understanding, or at least allow our emotions to better support our growth. Again, we wish to reinforce positive ones and transcend negative ones.

While we may find the seminar process sometimes difficult and challenging, eventually it will help us learn how to step outside of ourselves and, together with others, examine our lives. If we develop the courage to truly share ourselves, we discover others will not look down at the worst in us, but rather respect and trust our desire to be the best we can be and to realize our unique potential.

Seminar Structure

The size of seminars varies; time is the main factor impacted by size. Give people enough time to express themselves and get feedback from others, while still having enough people in the group to create a good level of synergy. Experience will teach the best balance.

Homework is often assigned for seminars. Homework provides us the opportunity to step out of the pressures and daily routine of our lives, and focus on our growth and ourselves. In the seminar, homework becomes an immediate way to focus on our deeper selves.

There are ten seminar guidelines that are read aloud to set the tone and context of synergy for every seminar. The group may then begin to seminar together or in subgroups by sharing homework and/or addressing personal growth issues. When the Hyde-Bath faculty "seminars," they usually do so by breaking out in smaller groups to give each person more time to share and receive feedback.

A facilitator is usually appointed to conduct the seminar; otherwise the group or subgroup selects one when the group is too large. While the facilitator shares from personal experience like all other seminar members, he or she is ultimately responsible for maintaining the integrity of the seminar. To handle difficult situations, he or she may ask for help from the group, but remains the final authority regarding the conduct of the seminar. This responsibility can be rotated each meeting among more experienced members who understand the seminar process.

It is well understood by all participants that the ultimate authority in any seminar is conscience.

The seminar time is usually one to two hours; however, special circumstances may lead members to change this. The time is divided equally among the members, first to share the given seminar focus, and then to receive responses. A timekeeper—not the facilitator—is selected to maintain the time frames.

The seminar is an important and serious undertaking. It should reflect discipline, openness, and honesty. The seminar tone is often deeply emotional, but punctuated by humor and our ability to laugh at ourselves.

The seminar atmosphere is usually intense and sometimes confrontational, but always marked by empathy and compassion.

Sometimes we may leave the seminar feeling emotionally spent, but also with a sense of fulfillment, hope, and determination. Often participants will share action steps they plan to take in order to follow up on what they learned. Participants usually commit to holding each other accountable for those steps.

The seminar room or space should be well lit and reasonably devoid of clutter. The seating arrangement should be circular so every participant can see everyone in the circle. Chairs, benches, and sofas are best, with some participants sitting on the floor if necessary.

No standing or lying down. Try to maximize how completely participants see each other (no desks or tables between) and minimize the distance from each other, without creating an outer circle. The facilitator must clearly see all and be visible to all, as should each participant.

The posture of participants is comfortable and relaxed, but always attentive. Taking notes may or may not be allowed, but it is not encouraged because it can interfere with the vital listening-and-responding process. Continual involvement and attention must be insisted upon. If the session is particularly intense, a short break might be useful. No side conversations. No food or alcohol; decide regarding beverages like coffee. No distractions. "Hyde time" is five minutes early, but on time is accepted. Quiet should occur immediately. Lateness should be addressed. Anyone with uncompleted homework may be asked to leave the seminar to complete it. Members of a newly formed group should introduce themselves, and newcomers should always introduce themselves. It is important to remind the group that each person is responsible for the seminar.

Since meetings are strictly confidential, members should know they can share personal information about themselves. It is a matter of personal integrity that each member never shares what goes on in seminar outside the meeting, although on campus, Hyde staff members may need to share with school leaders in order to maximize the growth process for each family.

The seminar begins with "Clearing the Decks." This means that members must share any concerns they have about other participants or about themselves that might interfere with their head-heart-soul openness in the seminar. If the concern is about another person, a participant would, at a minimum, indicate the concern and acknowledge a plan to discuss it with the individual after the meeting. There is no dialogue during this time. Clearing the Decks also signals dedication to the seminar process.

The facilitator explains the subject and the process of the seminar. A timekeeper is appointed, usually a volunteer, and the remaining time is divided by the number of participants. A brief time is generally saved for the end of the seminar so participants can share what they are getting out of the meeting. The participants read the seminar guidelines; sometimes short questions or comments about the guidelines are allowed to help clarify them.

Seminar Guidelines

1. When in doubt, I will bet on the truth; still in doubt, I will bet on more truth.
2. I will listen and not act defensively. (I cannot hear with my mouth open.)
3. I will not give advice, complain, explain, intellectualize, or protect. I will move from my Head through my Heart to my Soul.
4. I will be specific, speak for myself, and stay on the subject.
5. I will share from my own experiences. *I know how you feel. . . . I have felt the same way. . . . This is what I have found.*
6. I will stay out of my ego as much as I can. I will take my job seriously, not myself.
7. With my conscience as my guide, I will support and challenge the best from others in the group. I will let others know how I feel about them.
8. I have a personal obligation to make this seminar go.
9. I will try not to take comments personally. If the shoe fits, wear it; if not, throw it away.
10. What goes on in this room stays in this room. (There may be times, however, when an issue needs to be shared with school staff for the benefit of a student.)

Here are thoughts regarding each guideline:

1. Truth is the critical foundation of the Unifying process.
2. Listening is a fine Unifying art.
3. We are focused on our growth.
4. We are disciplined in what we share.
5. We focus on sharing our common experiences.
6. We are not self-serving in what we share.

7. We seek to be our best self to help others.
8. We all need to contribute to the seminar.
9. We all need to be open to help—useful or not.
10. Participants must respect confidentiality.

Finally, in order to help others as we have been helped, we learn to respond with our own experiences and emotions:

- Instead of giving advice to a participant, we try to respond with our own experiences that are similar to theirs: *I know how you feel; I have felt the same way myself, and this is what I found.* This humanizes our responses, and allows others to decide what they can apply from what we have shared.
- When we are really into the seminar, what others share will often reach our own feelings and emotions. By sharing in response, our sincerity and depth provide a powerful synergy, not only to that person, but also to the entire seminar group.

A final note: Unifying seminars go so deep they are sometimes seen by outsiders as therapeutic. A Unifying seminar is like any well-structured twelve-step program that gets deep without professionals.

7

RIGOR, SYNERGY, CONSCIENCE

Progressive Levels of Learning

The Unifying process is built on three developmental concepts: rigor, synergy, and conscience. Except for rigor as expressed in academic and military training, these concepts are largely unexplored by our present society, at least in a formal and explicit way. To illustrate: America was founded on principles of *individuality* and *equality*. America has honored the *individuality* part with our reverence that has been an inspiration to the entire world. But even our strongest supporters would admit we have yet to understand and appreciate, much less honor, the *equality* part. Equality has sometimes had to almost be shoved down our throats, as our women's suffrage and civil rights movements remind us.

The Unifying process transcends traditional American education by teaching us to appreciate equality as a powerful and essential step in realizing our unique potential. Where traditional education may lead us to worship the Rambo who prevails single-handedly, Unifying teaches us the superiority of the individual who achieves a higher best by being connected to others. This human connection of synergy helps us to find our deepest self and our conscience: the compass of our destiny.

The Unifying Rigor-Synergy-Conscience process is accomplished in three levels of growth that accumulate as we grow.

The *rigor* level reflects our striving to reach our best growth. It drives us to make the discovery of our unique potential a priority in our lives, and places it above our free will, our desire to control, and our desire to have life our own way. It drives us to discipline our inherent self-centeredness and our self-protection and self-gratification drives. It drives us to dedicate our lives to a sense of purpose.

The *synergy* level reflects our capacity to utilize the help of others to reach an even higher best in ourselves. Others can see our best and our unique potential in ways we ourselves cannot. Further, synergy empowers us to help others as we have been helped, a major step in expressing our purpose in life and our destiny. We become open with others at a deep level, and they in turn feel they can be open about themselves with us. It brings truth to the Golden Rule: Do unto others as you would have them do unto you.

The *conscience* level reflects the most advanced growth level, helping us develop our inner guidance system for life. Rigor helps us be our best selves; synergy exposes us to an even higher best and to an appreciation of the help of others; then conscience gives us the confidence to seek the truth wherever it may lead, and to do the right thing—the path to our destiny.

Conscience empowers us not only to hear our deepest inner voice, but to follow its lead.

Rigor, synergy, and conscience reflect developmental steps that operate in concert as we experience life.

LEVEL I: RIGOR

Developing Our Character Foundation

We are not put on this earth to drift and just dream. The value we place on rigor signifies the respect we have for ourselves and for our purpose in life. The decline and fall of the Roman Empire can be traced to the decline and fall of individual rigor. It should concern us that in our society today, rigor often seems focused on the military or serious research.

Rigor establishes the fundamentals of the character foundation, which begins in childhood under the leadership of the family.

Two truths establish an important discipline for all Unifying parents:

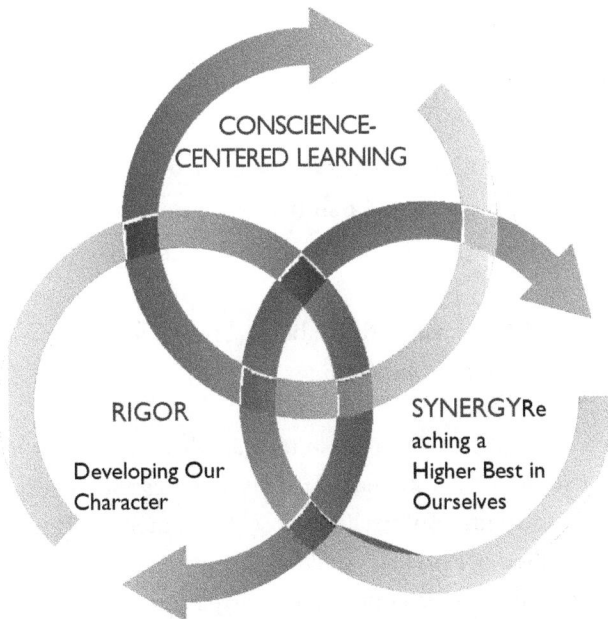

CONSCIENCE-
CENTERED LEARNING

RIGOR

Developing Our
Character

SYNERGYRe
aching a
Higher Best in
Ourselves

Rigor-Synergy-Conscience Stages of Growth. *Hyde School*

1. Character is primarily taught by example. Overall success primarily depends upon how well Unifying parents and teachers internalize the process both personally and as a parent or teacher. We teach it by example.
2. In character development, parents are the primary teachers and home is the primary classroom. The success of the Unifying student primarily depends upon how well the parent comes to understand and teach the process, and how well the process is ultimately practiced in the family and home.

Unifying parents and teachers continually ask: *How am I applying the process in my own life? In my parenting? In my family?* The rigor stage is highlighted by three essential Unifying ethics: Delayed Gratification, Never Lie–Never Quit, and Curiosity.

The Delayed Gratification Ethic

The crucial importance of teaching children delayed gratification in the development of character was resoundingly confirmed by "the marshmallow test," conducted by Stanford University in the 1960s. A group of four-year-olds was given the choice of one marshmallow now or two marshmallows later—if they would wait until the researcher conducting the experiment finished an "errand."

Dr. Daniel Goleman writes about this remarkable experiment in his book *Emotional Intelligence*:

> Some four-year-olds were able to wait what must surely have seemed an endless fifteen or twenty minutes for the experimenter to return. To sustain themselves in their struggle they covered their eyes so they wouldn't have to stare at temptation, or rested their heads in their arms, talked to themselves, sang, played games with their hands and feet, even tried to go to

sleep. These plucky preschoolers got the two-marshmallow reward. But others, more impulsive, grabbed the one marshmallow, almost always within seconds of the experimenter's leaving the room on his "errand."

The diagnostic power of how this moment of impulse was handled became clear some twelve to fourteen years later, when these same children were tracked down as adolescents. The emotional and social difference between the grab-the-marshmallow preschoolers and their gratification-delaying peers was dramatic.

Those who resisted temptation at four were now, as adolescents, more socially competent, personally effective, self-assertive, and better able to cope with the frustrations of life. They were less likely to go to pieces, freeze, or regress under stress, or become rattled and disorganized when pressured; they embraced challenges and pursued them instead of giving up even in the face of difficulties; they were self-reliant and confident, trustworthy, and dependable; and they took initiative and plunged into projects. And, more than a decade later, they were still able to delay gratification in pursuit of their goals.

The third or so who grabbed the marshmallow, however, tended to have fewer of these qualities, and shared instead a relatively more troubled psychological portrait. In adolescence they were more likely to be seen as shying away from social contacts; to be stubborn and indecisive; to be easily upset by frustrations; to think of themselves as "bad" or unworthy; to regress or become immobilized by stress; to be mistrustful and resentful about not "getting enough"; to be prone to envy and jealousy; to overreact to irritations with a sharp temper, so provoking arguments and fights. And, after all these years, they were still unable to put off gratification.

Even more surprisingly, when the tested children were evaluated again as they were finishing high school, those who had waited patiently at four were far superior as students to those who had acted on whim. According to their parents' evaluations, they were more academically competent: better able to put their ideas into words, to use and respond to reason, to concentrate, to make plans and follow through with them, and more eager to learn.

Most astonishingly, they had dramatically higher scores on their SAT tests. The third of the children who at four had grabbed for the marshmallow most eagerly had an average verbal score of 524 and quantitative (or "math") score of 528; the third who waited longest had average scores of 610 and 652, respectively—a 210-point difference in total score. [Note: the higher scores of both groups could be attributed to the fact they were mostly children of Stanford professors.]

This study makes it clear that the parents of the "waiters" had already begun to teach their children at age four how to transcend their lesser instincts, and that the parents of the "grabbers" had not.

Study the observation of the "waiters" when they became adolescents—socially competent, self-reliant and confident, more academically confident, and so on. We see the development of their deeper intellectual, emotional, and spiritual resources and, as they are able to transcend their lesser instincts, the beginning of their higher human self.

I have asked Hyde students (and their parents) how they might have reacted to the marshmallow test at age four. More than two-thirds of them agreed they would have grabbed the marshmallow—typical for kids who haven't been effectively trained in delaying their wants in order to achieve their high expectations. Hyde families all have high expectations, yet most of them were failing to teach their children this vital capacity needed to fulfill them.

So a major task should be teaching youngsters how to delay gratification. Self-discipline is a major part of the Unifying program—homework, chores, order, dress, timeliness, manners, respect, responsibilities. We cannot effectively do this without a dedicated effort by Unifying parents to model it for their children and practice it at home.

The entire Unifying program is about delaying gratification— preparing for your future rather than having life the way you want it, and trying to accomplish this personal development in a relatively short period of time.

A minority of parents today have taught their children the depth of self-discipline needed to help them realize their higher expectations in life. Parents should realize this need, and significantly step up their own delayed gratification efforts at home as a means to support their children's success in life.

The Never Lie–Never Quit Ethic

Another difficult preparation for incoming students is Unifying's Never Lie–Never Quit ethic. Because of the gap that has existed between expectations and actual performance (both academically and personally,) incoming students have often developed bad habits, in particular, lying and quitting.

Students who will lie under pressure create a public-self alien to their true spirit, and thus in time render their private (and true) selves a relatively ineffective force in their lives.

Adolescents have some crucial growth to accomplish; lying short-circuits their most powerful inner resources to experience this growth.

It is absolutely essential that Unifying students learn to take full responsibility for their actions and words. This enables them to focus on their true selves, to fully internalize right from wrong, and to gain a deep sense of confidence in how they deal with the

Captains of Lacrosse after Winning League Championship. ***Hyde School***

challenges of life. In time they will develop a powerful sense of integrity that will allow them to hear and be guided by conscience.

As little children, our egos are allowed to play around with truth and reality; adults encourage us to believe in Santa Claus and the tooth fairy, for example. This latitude with the truth is needed to help us see a larger perspective. Sometimes it helps us to test life beyond what we think is reality.

But in adolescence, we must learn to differentiate between daydreams and the development of potentially damaging self-deceptions and outright lies. A Unifying student describes this vital step:

> *I had been very dishonest my first year at Hyde, and while something deep down within me told me being dishonest was wrong, I was not sure why I necessarily had to be honest. There was no motivation in my life to be honest.*

One day, my eye caught a sign that read, "The truth will set you free, but first it will make you miserable." I realized right then why I wanted to be honest—I wanted to be free. Free from a life I was constantly dissatisfied with, and free from the wrong path I'd been on. From that point on, I have always asked, "How free am I?" And to find the answer, I look at how honest I am.

Note the clarity and depth with which this student is beginning to deal with his inner self. Clearly this experience signals that his higher human self-transcendence is in process.

Students who allow themselves to quit create a similar problem for their growth. Quitting gives in to lesser instincts, and begins to reinforce a comfortable self that will deny critical growth experiences.

It is essential that Unifying students do not allow their own feelings of fear, discomfort, or lack of confidence to control or influence how they deal with challenges. They need a belief in themselves that they will always finish what they start. In time this attitude empowers them to do things they never thought possible—as long as they don't quit on themselves.

Society today generally does a poor job in helping growing children confront lying and quitting attitudes; we have created a society that values achievement more than growth. Unifying values growth over achievement. Once parents understand why this ethic is fundamental, they can initiate a more meaningful Never Lie–Never Quit ethic in their own lives and homes.

Further, if we parents look hard enough, we can find areas where we should be more honest, or where we need more courage. It is the example of the changes we make in ourselves that will most powerfully influence our children's growth.

Make sure your family relationships are honest. If you don't believe your child in a given situation, say so. It is a statement that says either your child is not telling the truth or the two of you need to work on your relationship.

Lies are often cut-and-dry for us as adults. What may not be as clear, and thus very destructive, is our own expression of emotional dishonesty.

To understand this, children imitate parents from birth and thus develop primarily a visual, not a vocal, connection to caretakers: children learn to read our hearts (emotions), not our minds. This is why children are able to manipulate parents—while parents *think* they make a decision, the child can "hear" what the parent will actually ultimately do.

Children don't begin to think logically and abstractly until age eleven, but are experienced in imitating us from birth.

So to be effective, parents—and adults in general—*need to primarily learn to raise children by becoming living examples of growth.*

Since children read our hearts, our words and actions must be based on our beliefs and character, particularly our honesty about our strengths, challenges, and shortcomings.

Remember, our children have already internalized these things. By consciously sharing them, our strengths give them confidence, and our honesty about our challenges and shortcomings brings an integrity to both our and our children's lives. We also begin to help each other with the negative emotional dispositions (NEDs) we both internalized in early childhood from our parents, over which we had no control.

I first realized this natural connection from an episode when my nine-year-old son lied about giving a friend my old watch, which made his friend look like a thief. I was thunderstruck—how could he do that to a friend?

But eventually I realized that if we were going to take credit for our wonderful son, how could we not also take credit for his dishonesty?

So I searched for the dishonesty within myself and found it: I had always said to Malcolm, "I don't care how well you do, as long as it's your best." He had read my heart and knew it was a lie—no matter what I said, inwardly, I did care how well he did. His achievements—grades, athletics, college—mattered to me.

It took time to change myself so that my heart actually matched those words, but once I did, his lying went away. The more we model ourselves as living examples, the more we will connect with kids. What they really need is our experience and our concern.

The Curiosity Ethic

Finally, in addition to the Delayed Gratification and Never Lie–Never Quit ethics, we need to add a Curiosity ethic as one of our growth fundamentals. (We will discuss more about curiosity as the first step of Unifying's Pathway to Excellence in chapter 8. But curiosity here is simply a vital ethic we must continually practice.)

Curiosity is the foundation for the most powerful human motivation of all, self-discovery: *Who am I? Where am I going with my life? What do I need to get there?*

We must maintain a high sense of curiosity in order to grow. Sometimes when we don't understand something, we don't ask for fear of looking stupid. Sometimes we'd like to know people better, or ask why they did such and such, but we don't for fear of what they might think about us; the "why we don't ask" list is endless.

Since the growth of children will naturally be stunted to some degree by their self-protection and self-gratification lesser instincts, it is up to us as parents and teachers to find ways to challenge them with new experiences, new activities, new responsibil-

Joe Gauld with His Grandson Harrison, Who Has Autism, at His High School Graduation. *Hyde School*

ities, travel, and so forth. What they actually learn is less important than the rate of growth it will help them maintain.

These three ethics complete the rigor stage of growth, which we will continue throughout our Hyde Rigor-Synergy-Conscience continuum. The emphasis in the next stage is on synergy.

LEVEL 2: SYNERGY

Reaching a higher best in ourselves, synergy is $1 + 1 = 3$: your energy plus my energy creates an additional energy. A vital force in human development, synergy is perhaps the most underdeveloped resource in our society today. Others can see our best and our unique potential in ways we ourselves cannot. By learning to share our growth with others, we are able to find a higher best in ourselves.

Our survival and self-gratification lesser instincts are powerful. Consider our many addictions today—alcohol, drugs, tobacco, sex, food, power, shopping, and so on. Consider how our deeper emotional dispositions can control our attitudes and behavior. Consider that we are all creatures of habit. Realize the great challenge we each face in trying to control our lesser self in order to live a responsible and meaningful life.

But control will seldom solve the problem we have with our lesser instincts. They will always be a part of us, and we need them. What we must learn to do is utilize our deeper human resources to transcend them in our quest to fulfill our destiny in life.

For a prime example, take the alcoholic who, struggling with his addiction, finally realizes he is unable to "control" his drinking. So he tries to quit completely, but finds willpower fails him. Then, in desperation, he joins Alcoholics Anonymous and amazingly solves his problem through the help of others.

This demonstrates the power of synergy—together we create an additional energy, expressed in the deeper human quality of concern for others: we both want to quit drinking; we need our collective willpower to stay sober.

Synergy and concern—and other qualities of character—are powerful means to transcend our lesser self. By continual practice, the alcoholic ultimately develops a new life vastly superior to his alcoholic one. In essence, he never does control or solve his drinking problem; he simply transcends it.

Bill W., the founder of Alcoholics Anonymous, should be credited with discovering the power of synergy in human development. Like other alcoholics in his time, he struggled mightily and unsuccessfully to cure his addiction. Dedicated clergy, doctors, and psychiatrists shared his frustration of unsuccessfully helping alcoholics solve what is now termed a disease.

Finally, in the darkest moments of his struggle to recover from alcoholism, Bill had a creative moment when he convinced eventual AA cofounder Dr. Bob that together they had the strength to collectively solve their alcohol problem. Reluctantly, Dr. Bob agreed to try, and AA was born.

Today AA synergy is comparable to the effectiveness of the Salk vaccine in offering a surefire solution to alcoholics who truly commit to recovery. AA's success has spawned countless other self-help programs that utilize the power of synergy to solve various problems.

Yet, even today, the harnessing of synergy seems restricted to dealing with "problems," as if something has to be wrong before it can be formally applied. While there is increasing use of terms like "teamwork," "alliance," and "collaboration," which imply the value and power of synergy, synergy is yet to be formally associated with the concept of excellence in human development or in education.

But synergy, along with our own personal commitment to excellence, is what powers the Unifying process. Our lesser instincts and our egos help form habits, attitudes, and emotional dispositions that may be counterproductive to our character growth. Synergy can inspire our deeper intellectual, emotional, and spiritual resources to transcend them.

Something that has always puzzled me all my life is why, when I am in special need of help, the good deed is usually done by somebody on whom I have no claim. —William Feather

LEVEL 3: CONSCIENCE

Conscience-centered learning is the most advanced level in the Unifying process. It completes our lesser self to higher human self-transformation in which we develop our deeper intellectual, emotional, and spiritual resources, enabling us to hear our conscience and follow its dictates and direction. This advanced learning level requires us to learn to distinguish between our inner voices of ego and conscience. Our ego begins to form virtually at birth, programming our responses in life. For example, we learn to react to praise with feelings of joy and perhaps a smile, while criticism leads to hurt and possibly crying. In essence, our ego is often rooted in our initial lesser instincts of self-protection, self-gratification, and self-centeredness.

But in our teen years, our character development begins in earnest, which gives us the capability of transcending our lesser selves, and opens us to the deeper and more powerful voice of conscience.

Teenagers can feel beset by two voices, one continuing to urge the pursuit of more primitive wants, and the newer, softer voice counseling truth and a larger purpose. How well teenagers are able to distinguish the two voices measures their intellectual character, and how well their actions follow conscience—the compass of our destiny—measures their moral character.

Our rigor and synergy stages of development have prepared us for this deeper conscience-centered learning stage.

- Our Delayed Gratification ethic has enabled us to transcend our initial self-protection and self-gratification instincts in order to develop our deeper potentials and our character.
- Our Never Lie–Never Quit ethic has enabled our deeper inner selves and our unique potential to lead our lives.
- Our Curiosity ethic has enabled us to focus on the three basic questions: *Who am I? Where am I going? What do I need to get there?*

- Synergy has enabled us to transcend our inherent self-centeredness by learning how to utilize the help of others, and then to help others as we have been helped.

In addressing our habits, attitudes, and emotional dispositions, we have reaffirmed those family and childhood experiences that enhance the development of our deeper selves, while transcending our counterproductive attitudes and emotional dispositions. Now the Five Principles and the Five Words further empower our conscience-based learning.

Hyde-Bath seniors spend fifty hours in the spring term in conscience-centered learning. To the extent they master rigor and synergy, their sharing sessions with classmates and faculty enable them to understand their deepest selves—and the leadership of conscience. As Sigmund Freud wisely noted, we humans usually make our most important decisions—like choosing a mate or a career—at this deeper level.

As I said, our egos are like the sergeant in the trenches—helping make our day-to-day decisions. But conscience is like the general knowing the entire war plan—guiding our life decisions and our destiny.

We all seek to control our lives with a strong intellectual/rational emphasis in our decisions. This places our egos in control. Meanwhile, the power of our subconscious—insight, intuition, conscience—is in overdrive. One study gave two groups a complex problem to address. They then interrupted one group with a different problem to work on. The solution of that group to the original problem ultimately proved superior, indicating that giving their subconscious time to address the problem led to success.

Other studies suggest the subconscious' greater power. But we live in a world that worships the intellect's wisdom, neatly declaring truth as something that is *logically* proven, dismissing all else as unproven mystery or myth.

Here is how the Unifying program describes conscience: Conscience is the deepest sense of self-consciousness, the awareness that our decisions make us authentic. It is our capacity to know right from wrong. Conscience goads us to align our actions with our beliefs about what is truly worthwhile, giving us a sense of integrity or wholeness.

We need to distinguish within ourselves an ego self and a higher self, or two types of emotions and feelings that motivate our actions:

- *Self-regarding emotions* are motivations that prompt us to act on our likes and dislikes, our desires and fears.
- *Self-transcending emotions* are motivations that prompt us to go beyond ourselves and seek what is truly worthwhile: truth, beauty, excellence, noble deeds, respect for individuals, love, destiny.

The development of our character helps bring our self-regarding emotions into alignment with our self-transcending emotions.

Our character is developed by the Action-Reflection Learning Cycle. We grow by thoughtfully reflecting on our actions and motives and then continually repeating the cycle.

We find this foundation makes us sensitive to conscience, and conscience becomes the guiding force to help us realize our unique potential—our source for a meaningful and fulfilling life.

Conscience-centered learning completes our transformation into our higher human self. It inspires us to seek the truth wherever it may lead and to recognize and do the right thing. It introduces us to a treasure chest of deeper and more spiritual resources.

Conscience-centered learning inspires:

- A sense of purpose and an enthusiasm for life and learning
- A depth of faith that elevates our courage to a new level
- A genuine confidence in ourselves and our unique potential
- An active concern for the welfare of others and commitment to their best
- A deep trust in the leadership of conscience and in spiritual guidance

We are now ready to address the understanding and skill of the teacher to facilitate and administer the Unifying academic program.

8

UNIFYING ACADEMICS
Pathway to Excellence

It is clear that America's concerns and dissatisfaction with its education system have been both long and deep. The educational reforms to address those concerns—beginning in 1957 with Sputnik—have offered no relief or hope of change.

Parents Join with Teachers in a Seminar. *Hyde School*

The system was designed to teach literacy and knowledge. While it may seem to fit the traditions of older institutions, it does not well serve the very dynamic philosophy and values set down by America's founding fathers: equality—we all have dignity and worth; and individuality—we each need to develop our character, initiative, and creativity.

American children need an education that will emphasize these founding qualities and values, which in turn becomes a natural and stronger way to develop literacy and knowledge. First things first: make kids strong individuals and they will become strong students.

The academic core subjects—English, math, history, science, foreign language, the arts—have been the foundation of schooling for centuries. They have distinguished the learned person, the aristocrat, the gentleman, the lady, and the professional. The mastery of this curriculum has denoted one's enlightenment and culture, elevating an individual from the masses.

But the American commitment to equality challenged the elite nature of this education. To reaffirm our belief in the dignity and worth of all individuals, we sought to fully educate every American. The public school became our great hope to bring to every child the enlightenment and culture societies had previously reserved for the privileged few.

Today, the pervasive inequality that abounds in our educational system remains a painful bone in America's throat. While the American college and university system is acknowledged as the world's best, the academic achievement of public schools lags behind that of many other developed nations. Between 2017 and 2019, on National Assessment of Educational Progress (NAEP) reading tests, US fourth-grade scores dropped in seventeen states and improved in just one, and eighth-grade scores dropped in thirty-one states and improved in just one. Fourth-graders were 35 percent proficient and eighth-graders 34 percent proficient.[1]

Seventy-six percent of our high school graduates were found "not adequately academically."[2]

Given our computer and information age, this inherent inequality of opportunity is helping turn America into opposing divisions of "haves" and "have-nots," not unlike the societal gaps that led to the French and Russian Revolutions.

We believe this troubling problem is rooted in the inherent elitism of the ancient educational system. This system does not fit America.

Perhaps the best evidence is this: the top US student group, according to standardized tests, comprises the two million home school students, who by ninth grade generally score three grades higher than both public and private school students. And they accomplish this with only half of their teachers certified, and averaging $600 per student, versus $11,700 per public school student.[3]

The teaching of academic subjects today is not much different from how they were taught centuries ago to just the chosen few. Students then generally came from academically or financially advantaged families; thus, the teaching of subjects *assumed* this inherent preparation of students—as it still does today. So students who don't come from academically oriented homes—or who aren't born with academically oriented minds—are immediately disadvantaged, and unless their parents have money to buy additional academic help, they will generally experience school as an uphill battle. Some students do have the academic talent to make up for these background handicaps, but such students are a small minority. Students not born into some combination of advantages may yet become successful in life, but most do it in spite of our present educational system.

The inherent inequality of the American educational system ultimately penalizes *all* students. By unwittingly making the *achievement of knowledge* the goal, education simply becomes a superficial means to get the grade, get into college, or get a diploma. This achievement emphasis turns education into a horse race, teaching students to value what they *know*, rather than *who they are*. It undermines the primary purpose of education, to "know thyself," as championed by the ancient Greeks, and the quest to answer the three fundamental questions of true growth: *Who am I? Where am I going with my life? What do I need to get there?*

We believe a strong academic background is an essential building block in the development of one's unique potential and destiny. We further believe that every student, with the possible exception of the severely learning disabled, is capable of academic excellence that will facilitate the fulfillment of a larger purpose in life. However, to meet this higher educational goal requires a major transformation in America's present elitist approach to teaching academic subjects.

A deeper look at American education today reveals these disturbing realities:

- Motivation is the foundation of learning, yet most American students are poorly motivated to do serious academic work. Until this crucial issue of student motivation is successfully addressed, little academic improvement is possible.
- The major emphasis is on test scores and grades, with students focused on getting into college or on simply obtaining a diploma to enhance job opportunities, not on a deeper purpose of self-discovery. Hence, cheating has become a way of school life, and students retain little of what they learn in school.

- Our present educational system has never been able to reconcile *excellence* with *equality*. Attempts to raise academic standards inevitably lead to cries of elitism, and then attempts to reach all students bring cries of mediocrity. So American education ends up with pockets of excellence in "a rising tide of mediocrity."

These issues must be fully addressed before America can make any real educational progress. We believe the Unifying academic curriculum takes a major step in the right direction.

THE UNIFYING ACADEMIC CURRICULUM

The Hyde School was founded in 1966 to explore a new education based on this premise: "Every individual is gifted with a unique potential that defines a destiny." This was to be supported by a new curriculum focused on the development of character, specifically Curiosity, Courage, Concern for others, Leadership, and Integrity.

In 1970, the visiting committee for accreditation unanimously declared Hyde's educational experiment a success, stating that "older institutions could learn something from this relatively new school . . . that if character can be developed, then academic achievement up to the level of one's potential will follow."

So Hyde's academic approach became "Take care of the character, and the academics will follow." While Hyde did establish an enviable track record in college placements—97 percent of its graduates have gone on to four-year colleges—we became very concerned that we were not generating the same level of enthusiasm and excellence in our academic courses that we did in athletics, performing arts, and other areas of the program.

So in 1985, under the leadership of Dr. John Young, the Hyde Academic Advisory Committee began the challenge of finding a new curriculum that truly inspired academic excellence in our students. Thanks to the tireless and brilliant dedication of Dr. Young, together with the help of others, this program came to fruition in October 1995, just ten years after the work began. We present an overview here.

Academic Grading System

Since Hyde makes a major departure from traditional academic programs, it has always assigned students two academic grades: (1) achievement—basically the same as traditional education for the benefit of higher education; and (2) effort—based on the student's work responsibility and attitude, essentially measuring the percentage of his or her best.

The Purpose of Academics

It might be said that the basic purpose of a traditional curriculum today is to teach students academic skills and knowledge in preparation for further learning about life. In contrast, the purpose of the Unifying academic curriculum is *to help each student develop a broad personal understanding that will ultimately lead to the fulfillment of his or her unique potential and destiny.* In essence, while traditional education seeks to directly prepare students for the complexities of life, a Hyde education seeks to filter all student learning through the complexities of the inner self.

The Unifying educational process, centered on the belief in unique potential, further reinforces that we are all endowed with a *conscience* that serves as the compass of our destiny. So as each of us develops our comprehensive intellectual, physical, social, emotional, and spiritual (IPSES) resources (using the Action-Reflection Learning Cycle), we get closer to expressing our conscience. This learning process begins with an action, behavior, or experience, leading us to reflect on our identity in light of that action, behavior, or experience, which then leads us to take a certain view of ourselves. As we accept this new view of ourselves, we act in accordance with it, which leads us to repeat the learning cycle once again. Thus, the Action-Reflection Learning Cycle creates a perpetual chain of growth.

Clearly then, our learning capacity depends first on the depth and scope of the challenges we experience, and then on the depth and scope of our reflections on these challenges. We all can understand how, say, backing down from a challenge may stunt our growth, but do we also understand how our inability to effectively reflect upon our experiences may hurt us just as much?

I was a poor student in high school and was flunking geometry until my stepfather took over my instruction. He forced me to explain everything I wrote or said—a very frustrating learning experience. But I began to understand geometry and the possibility that my school performance might be due more to my lazy learning and reflection skills than to my average academic abilities.

The next year in math, on my first exam, I had every answer wrong, but Mr. Moulton (an excellent teacher) gave me an A-minus! I was so curious I finally risked asking him if he had made a mistake. He confirmed the grade, saying, "Yes, you need to work on your carelessness, but you know what you're doing."

Before these two experiences, I had assumed I simply had no talent for school, and I acted accordingly. But when my stepfather rigorously challenged my mind, the experience led me to rethink this perception of myself. Then Mr. Moulton's teaching skill helped me confirm that I could, in fact, think at a deeper level.

But it took both my stepfather's challenge *and* my reflections to change my math performance in school.

If *destiny* reflects our larger purpose in life, then *unique potential* represents our innate ability to fulfill it. In essence, then, we are faced with two major lifetime explorations: (1) to understand life, and indeed the universe, so we can realize what our own contribution is supposed to be (destiny); and (2) to understand ourselves and our deeper potentials so we can realize how to make that contribution (unique potential). Actually, these two explorations work in concert; that is, understanding life helps to reveal ourselves, and understanding ourselves helps to reveal our larger purpose in life. Contrary to traditional education, the Unifying process insists that both these inner and outer explorations are to be emphasized and done together.

Further, we believe a strong academic foundation is essential to freeing students from the inherent limitations of their particular backgrounds and environments, which in turn will help them take the largest possible view of both themselves and life.

Our families, plus people, events, and circumstances in our growing up, profoundly influence both the direction and the nature of our lives. However, a carefully structured academic program can expose us to larger truths, so we can (1) better appreciate the strengths of these growing-up influences while (2) transcending those shortcomings that restrict the development of our unique potential-destiny path in life.

Some years ago in a Philippine jungle, a primitive tribe was discovered that, untouched by civilization, had a culture that was remarkably unchanged over thousands of years. The tribe had been held a virtual prisoner of itself. (Some would say its members were lucky to avoid the rest of us!)

To some degree, we all share similar restrictions in our own personal growth. Before my stepfather's intervention, my teachers and I had obviously created an Action-Reflection Learning Cycle that reaffirmed school was not for me. My stepfather's brilliant intervention helped to lift me beyond this restrictive cycle; this and other experiences ultimately led me to discover that my destiny was, in fact, located in schoolwork!

The Hyde academic program is designed to give students the opportunity to look more deeply at themselves and life. English and math give us the personal tools to understand and express our unique potential; science and history reveal the human and natural environments in which our destiny will take place, and foreign language helps us transcend our specific culture to see our unique potential-destiny in a different context. The arts importantly give us the opportunity to express our deeper selves.

English: English provides us with a deeper understanding of the thoughts and feelings of others, which often draws from us a clearer sense of ourselves. This identification process, together with the disciplined communication skills English can demand from us, allows us to contribute to the growth of others, and our contributions then become a vital means for our own growth. The process of journaling in particular can help teach us to understand and express our deeper selves and our conscience, and give us insight into our own unique potential.

Mathematics: "The purest form of logic known to man" helps us to organize and sharpen our thinking skills. It leads us to confront our biases and misperceptions, and to more clearly understand our ideas and beliefs. The theory of numbers itself develops our ability to grasp complexities and thus contributes to our leadership capabilities.

Science: Science provides us with an in-depth look at how the process of life actually works and the basic truths that seem to govern the Earth and the universe. This provides us with the physical framework in which our destinies will be expressed. The scientific method of exploration itself provides us with a discipline to further our own self-discovery.

History: History allows us to study the pattern of how societies have expressed their collective destinies to create civilizations, and how individuals in particular have influenced mankind's direction. This panorama provides the human framework to express our own purpose in life. American history specifically helps us to become part of the great American experiment that commits us to the development of the dignity and worth of all individuals.

Foreign language: Foreign language offers us a deeper understanding of the world's cultural diversity, as well as the opportunity to reflect upon ourselves and our own position in the world. A language can offer insights into a specific culture different from our own.

The arts: The arts provide a number of diverse activities in which we can open ourselves to express our heart and soul. Our work can be appreciated for its beauty or emotional power and can, on one hand, express our imagination or creativity, and on the other, our technical skill.

FOUR FUNDAMENTALS OF INTELLECTUAL CHARACTER

Our growth depends on the Action-Reflection Learning Cycle: we act, think about it, then act once again. Excellence in this process requires not just our best actions, but also our best thinking. So if our actions reflect our *moral character*, which we define by Curiosity, Courage, Concern for others, Leadership, and Integrity, then our thinking reflects our *intellectual character*.

This concept of intellectual character can lead us to a powerful new approach to academic excellence, replacing the traditional and limiting emphasis on achievement.

In traditional education, the teacher establishes the criteria that will evaluate the student's understanding of the material, leading to a grade that measures the student's "achievement." While the student's attitude and effort—qualities like curiosity, hard work, perseverance, cooperation, attentiveness, insightfulness—obviously affect the student's achievement, they do so indirectly. In fact, Rob, a very bright student who chooses to be lazy, uninterested, and self-centered, might actually achieve a much higher grade than Phil, a "plugger" who has developed all of the excellent character qualities listed above. Whether we Americans like it or not, inborn ability plays the major role in academic achievement.

However, once the goal becomes the development of one's unique potential and destiny, clearly Phil's character begins to set the new standard, while Rob's attitude and effort indicate serious growth problems, regardless of how exceptional his academic abilities might be. For if we focus on unique potential instead of academic achievement, each one of us becomes "exceptional" rather than just the academically gifted few. So what begins to actually distinguish us in our education is how exceptional our character becomes. Thus, unique potential levels the educational playing field and puts excellence within the reach of every student.

In the traditional achievement system, the primary concern is what the student *knows*, with emphasis on the student's achievement. In a unique potential-destiny system, the primary concern becomes who the student *is*, with emphasis on how the student acts and reflects. This new focus puts the premium on both *intellectual and moral character*, and both of these reflect *learned* behaviors and attitudes that largely transcend our inborn abilities.

Hyde's overall approach to academic learning is a departure from the traditional emphasis on achievement.

AICR: UNIFYING ACADEMIC PRACTICES

Intellectual character reflects our thinking, attitudes, and efforts and can be seen as our *habitual disposition* to seek the truth, whatever it is. We learned that the foundation of our intellectual character is built by rigorously developing excellence in these four sequential thinking attitudes: (1) Be Attentive, (2) Be Insightful, (3) Be Critical, and (4) Be Responsible. We refer to these as AICR, pronounced "acre."

Be Attentive

The first step in thinking effectively comes with learning to discipline our minds to the task at hand. Do we have the capacity to rivet our attention on the lesson? Can we blot out distractions during homework, class, or other activities? Do we focus well enough to hear nuances or read between the lines? I think most of us would be shocked by the relative ineffectiveness of our listening or reading awareness. Clearly a high attentiveness quotient is essential to thinking excellence.

The vignettes describe the students' understanding of the *Be Attentive* part of the academic learning cycle.

> *Mrs. G in 7th grade social studies was the strictest teacher I ever had. She made me stay after school for Friday's detentions until I got my missing assignments done. She also taught us how to take good notes. She had open-note tests that would be impossible to do without notes, and she never let me take the test when I didn't have my notes. I think that her strictness,*

work ethic, and understanding of unique potential made her the closest teacher I ever had to Hyde teaching. I really hated her; now I think she was one of the best teachers I ever had before Hyde.

Mrs. B teaches with enthusiasm and knowledge of the subject, which gets you interested. She also creates an environment where you are not comfortable not being prepared, or if your assignments don't reflect your best effort. This makes everyone work harder.

Mrs. K taught me to be a tough athlete and to never give up. Her teaching and belief have so much to do with my own commitment; this year I see my improvement in soccer and I am proud of myself.

In history, Mr. W can get our entire class focused with a touch or eye contact; when we don't pay attention, he will casually get up and start walking on tables, still talking like nothing was different. One day when we were studying Karl Marx, he came dressed up and acted like Karl Marx the whole period. It helped me see and feel the essence of history.

Every day, Ms. H has the entire class write five major points that were covered the previous day.

In ceramics, I was inspired by an expert potter who came to our class. I was deeply touched by all the ideas he gave us. I learned how to make pots quickly, how to shape pots, as well as learning the basics better (for example: centering). For a few weeks, all I thought about was pottery.

My first day, I was shocked by Mr. D's enthusiasm. He was jumping around the room; he actually jumped out the window.

He keeps people attentive, gets in your face, moves around a lot, and uses different voice levels. Although he was very intimidating, I learned my lessons by paying attention. He also helped me build my confidence by forcing me to speak loud enough so everyone could hear me.

You never know what's going to happen next in Mr. H's class. He could call someone on their attitude, or ask you a question he thinks you might not know. He constantly has you on your toes, which gets you to keep yourself in check in terms of your attention and your attitude.

In Mrs. G's English class, she always came in completely prepared and motivated. She never wasted any time. She always asked the class for input. Her projects were unique and thought-provoking. She was willing to stop the class to deal with an attitude. She always gave everyone feedback. She was fair and always open for extra help.

Be Insightful

How deeply do we think? Do we like to try to figure it out for ourselves? How often does our curiosity become aroused? Do we look to connect lessons to other truths? Do we strive to find the bigger picture? Do we seek new challenges to our minds? Adding this insightful nature to our thinking will better help us discover the path of our destinies. I think of a student who had failed two years of math but went on to get a PhD and write a book on computers that he dedicated to me for "teaching [him] the joys of Algebra."

Student vignettes help describe the *Be Insightful* part of AICR.

In English, Mr. C takes three questions—"Who am I? Where am I? What do I want to be?"—and teaches these through the material and himself. Everyone is either excited or fearful about themselves, so people become motivated to learn.

Mr. A makes Geometry class exciting by giving students ownership. One time he went to the board and drew nine dots in the shape of a square, telling us it was possible to connect all nine dots with four straight lines without taking the chalk off the board. Then he drew the solution which went outside the nine dots! He made me think of approaching other things from a larger picture.

In biology, Mr. G allows us to either completely focus on, or stray from, something depending on how we understand it and how things relate to each other. We spent two weeks on just cellular respiration, and took time to stray and learn about why starved people's bellies bloat. He also focuses on a couple of kids each day to make sure they really get called on and that they are 100% attentive. He trusts us to get our work done.

One day, Miss C took our ninth-grade class out for a hike. She told us only to think about the nature around us and how we live with it. We were all surprised and confused. There was no talking, and off we went in our separate ways. It was a beautiful and historic country. I felt like the only person alive. I walked through the grassy hills and sat in the middle of an ancient cemetery. All I thought about was life—how precious it is. Something hit me that day; I felt peaceful. At the time, my life wasn't going so well; it helped me change the way I was leading my life.

When we were first given an assignment to write a poem in French, I was intimidated. I barely knew any words in French, but it allowed us to be creative and express ourselves as well as learn French. We used art and language to express our feelings about autumn. I saw I could actually write a poem in French, and it also taught me descriptive verbs and adjectives I might not have learned otherwise.

In English, Mrs. G would try to relate many seemingly non-related things to show the connection that simple themes have. This helped me to apply little pieces of my own experience to other parts of my life. It taught me to apply that same attitude when I was struggling in my life.

Writing my autobiography in English was the most emotional situation I have ever encountered at Hyde. I wrote about fifteen pages that showed me how creative I could be and it helped me to evaluate my life. I later found myself filling in situations which I had blocked out over time. It was an enthusiastic and motivating way to work on my writing skills.

Be Critical

How important to us is knowing the truth? How dependent are we on the teacher or the help of others? Are we likely to find the error in the textbook, the lecture, or the class discussion? How sensitive are we to our own biases, prejudices, or shortcomings? How sensitive are we to those in others? Are we diligent in our learning and can we persevere? This kind of critical thinking capacity can measure our commitment to the truth.

Student vignettes describe the *Be Critical* phase of AICR.

In Mr. M's "freedom and responsibility" class, we were instructed to debate either the pros or cons of whether a dress code restricted our individuality. Once we had finished debating, Mr. M told us to switch and debate the other side. It taught us that to fully understand your own beliefs, you often have to look on the other side of it. It forced me to look at things from a perspective other than my own.

In biology, Mr. G makes objectives for each chapter, which really gets us focused. Through answering written questions and reading the chapters, we truly learn it for ourselves. Then during the week, he teaches more in-depth what we are already learning for ourselves. He makes us responsible for the bulk of the learning, and then he helps us make connections. He does this by putting the responsibility to learn on us. He makes it fun to learn because of the connections he makes.

In English, Mr. B doesn't just teach us; we all learn together from discussing things and seeing everyone's perspective. He allows us to freely express ourselves and our ideas in our writing; we also share everything we write, so we can see where everyone is and offer criticism.

I was an intern in summer school, and a student I was talking to said something like, "I don't care about myself." I replied, "I understand what you mean." I began to tell her about her good traits. A day later I made a list in my journal of my own good qualities. Since then I have focused on myself, not the things I don't like or wish to be different. Of course I constantly have things to work on, but rather than feeling hopeless about them, I look forward to what I can do.

In history, I was affected by the comparisons of children's books on Columbus; the misleading facts from the storybook stunned me. Myth and legends covered up what really happened during the discovery of America. This exercise showed me that you have to be a student of history, not a history student.

*The most fundamental development in my writing was my least
favorite. I had a storytelling style in my writing. Mr. R tore all
my papers apart, which was a huge check of humility for me. I
had always been one of the best writers in all my classes, and to
be criticized so redundantly was not in the least bit familiar. I
went through some dreadful stages of feeling hopeless and curs-
ing English forever. But by June I began to develop an analyti-
cal style of writing that felt more and more like my own. This
year I feel assured of my writing ability and I am grateful for
the high expectations that were put upon me.*

We have now taken three crucial steps in developing our intellectual character. We have been attentive, disciplining our mind to
the task at hand. We have been insightful, exploring all aspects of
this task. We have been critical, rigorously sorting out the main
body of truth. But now comes the most crucial step of all, the
essential payoff, as well as the real report card of our intellectual
efforts.

Be Responsible

How thoughtfully, and how committedly, do we act upon what we
have learned? It is one thing to follow the truth wherever it leads;
it is quite another to then do what we truly believe is genuinely
worthwhile. Do we have the courage of our convictions? Do our
acts reaffirm our words? Do we challenge ourselves to follow
through? Are we willing to risk mistakes, even failure? Do we look
forward to this step as a means to repeat the Action-Reflection
Learning Cycle once again?

Student vignettes describe the *Be Responsible* phase of AICR.

Mr. S placed us in groups on our very first day of Algebra II. I've been placed in groups before, but I've never had to be responsible for the others. We were all frustrated with this, but in time we realized that he was not just getting out of teaching, but rather making us take learning into our hands. You could still ask Mr. S for help, but you couldn't expect him to volunteer himself.

The "design your own lab" project was the hardest problem-solving I've ever done. It required us to build everything from hypothesis to experiment from scratch.

Our English class was struggling. Mr. M made us meet outside class and write a class commitment. We outlined our homework responsibilities and basic class requirements. We had ownership.

In Mrs. G's algebra class we had an exercise one day where we were given a topic and then we had to go to the front of the room and sell the class with as much enthusiasm as possible. The class was much closer after this, and we worked better together, because we had gained respect for each other.

Mr. H noted that while I had made progress, I had a lot of attitudes and issues that were untouched, and as a senior, "going through the motions" was unacceptable. Instead of trying to convince Mr. H to let me stay as a senior, I got belligerent, figuring that he already made the decision. He then told me the ball was in my court, and "what did I want to do with it?" Later I realized I needed to take responsibility for my attitude, and that it was up to me to change myself.

In Spanish, we were put in groups of five, and got to pick our own topic to present to the class. Our group fooled around and procrastinated, waiting until the last minute to put it together. We had the right information, but none of us learned the material. The next day we had a test on all the topics and I hardly got any of my own questions right. My whole group knew we did not work well together, and we knew the next time we had to work harder and challenge ourselves.

In biology, we had this project called mushroom/lichen "dating game." We went out and foraged for mushrooms, and then had to write creative ideas for ways of stating facts. We had to organize the project ourselves, budget our time, and be responsible for it. It greatly improved my research skills.

Mr. Mac sort of set a trap for me in geometry. He knew that I was very intellectually arrogant, and he was willing to confront it. He told me to move through the book at my own speed, that I didn't have to go at the speed of the class. We set up a curriculum and I had to follow that instead. I ended up behind, because I wasn't really motivated and didn't know the material as well as I pretended. He set up a situation that helped me realize that on my own.

Being in a group in math has kept me accountable for learning the material well, and also given me an opportunity to help others out. Our group has a powerful dynamic; we trust each other, give each other encouragement, and depend on each other for help and guidance. It also creates a bond in the class.

I gained a great deal in terms of organization, planning, and creative thought by being involved in the Greek play project assigned by Mrs. B. I was the coordinator of my group's play. It took much more work than I had anticipated, but it was also a great deal of fun.

Everything was going downhill, and I finally decided to go out on my own. I did end up keeping in touch with the headmaster, and the one sentence in a letter from him that stuck out in my head was, "Are you being an independent person, or just mimicking what an independent person does?" That made me think of what I was really doing.

These four steps are the pathway to self-discovery. They make us an *intentional learner* instead of just an incidental one, and help form the foundation for our intellectual and our moral character.

THE PATHWAY TO EXCELLENCE

We have now prepared ourselves to begin an exciting new approach to the traditional academic curriculum. The five words on the Hyde shield—Courage, Integrity, Concern, Curiosity, and Leadership—have always measured the excellence of a Unifying education. They inspire the beliefs, dedication, and pride of Hyde students. Their power is reaffirmed by the fact that Hyde graduates believe in them more strongly once they actually experience life—living proof of Heraclitus's prophetic statement: "Character is destiny."

In the past, these Unifying words have carried more meaning to Hyde students outside the classroom, particularly in challenging activities like athletics and performing arts. But now we are ready to center the Hyde academic curriculum as a primary and continuing way for students to develop Curiosity, Courage, Concern, Leadership, and Integrity.

These words now come to represent the five steps in Unifying's *Pathway to Excellence:*

1. Curiosity: *I am a learner.* I begin by accepting myself as a dynamic learner, always searching for the *truth* about myself and life.
2. Courage: *I learn the most about myself by accepting challenges.* I come to recognize that I must continually reach beyond myself to discover my best, the primary means to unlock my *destiny.*
3. Concern: *I need a challenging and supportive community to develop my character.* In my striving, I learn in *humility* that it takes the help of others to truly find my best.
4. Leadership: *I am a leader by asking the best of myself and others.* I come to realize a primary means for my growth is found in my *Brother's/Sister's Keeper* responsibility to help others as I have been helped.
5. Integrity: *I am gifted with a unique potential, and conscience is my guide in discovering it.* My dedication to learning deepens my appreciation of my unique potential and reveals my *conscience,* the compass to my destiny.

The steps of the Unifying's Pathway to Excellence are built on the Five Words: Curiosity, Courage, Concern, Leadership, and Integrity. As we study the five steps, we realize that they also reaffirm the Five Principles: Destiny, Humility, Conscience, Truth, and Brother's/Sister's Keeper.

The Pathway to Excellence transforms traditional education and begins to develop a personal academic excellence in students. It is designed to reach the deepest motivation in students.

In in-depth interviews, I have often been awed to hear students express this universal hope and dream: "To be the best I can be, to help other people, and to leave the world a better place." The Pathway to Excellence helps students approach academic rigor with the reassurance that no matter how difficult or uninteresting it may seem to be, it represents our best efforts to help youngsters fulfill their own sense of a larger purpose in life. This raises their spirit above the more superficial ego drive of simply getting better grades as a pipeline to better colleges and higher-paying jobs. All students can learn to become excellent in being attentive, insightful, critical, and responsible en route to fulfilling the five steps on the Pathway to Excellence. This importantly reaffirms their deep sense of justice that no student has either an unfair advantage or disadvantage in relationship to other students.

Understanding the pathway generates self-confidence and self-respect, because students know that they themselves—not their innate abilities—have truly earned their academic excellence. And thanks to the process of really *earning* their academic achievements, they are likely to retain a high percentage of what they have actually learned in school—in contrast to students retaining little of what they learn in traditional education.

In the Pathway to Excellence, students come to realize that the act of cheating and similar shortcuts will simply short-circuit their own hard-earned learning process, and in the long run ultimately hurt themselves.

The Pathway to Excellence puts academic fulfillment and excellence within the reach of every American youngster, regardless of academic talent or background. At the same time, it frees the more academically agile students and can challenge them to new heights. The Pathway to Excellence can create an educational environment that maximizes the academic growth—and achievement—of all.

NOTES

1. National Center for Education Statistics, "Reading Scores De-cline on 2019 Nation's Report Card," PRNewswire, October 30, 2019, https://www.prnewswire.com/news-releases/reading-scores-decline-on-2019-nations-report-card-300947739.html.

2. Gordon Crews, *Handbook of Research on School Violence in American K–12 Education* (Hershey, PA: IGI Global, 2019).

3. Brian D. Ray, "Homeschooling: The Research," National Home Education Research Institute, January 15, 2021, jnheri.org/research-facts-on-homeschooling.

Part III

Advancing the Unifying Process to Excellence

9

THE UNIFYING FAMILY LEARNING CENTER

Since the family is at the core of the Unifying process, this chapter is primarily addressed to parents, but it can help students gain

All Faculty and Students Create and Perform a Show for Spring Parents Weekend. *Hyde School*

a better understanding of what parents and family are contributing to student growth, as well as recognize those areas where young people compensate for parent and family shortcomings. Unifying teachers need to understand this chapter in order to effectively develop, teach, and manage the Unifying process.

We realize that for public schools, this chapter on family learning may be difficult to implement, particularly since very few schools presently involve parents and family in their educational process in a significant way. But we hope this will serve as a starting point, and begin to make educators aware on a deeper level of how to assist parents and families.

The massive 1966 "Coleman Report," the biggest study ever done on American public schools, was popularly summarized this way: Schools don't matter; families do.[1]

Just as nature's cocoon transforms the caterpillar into a butterfly, the family primarily transforms children from their initial lesser self into their higher human self. This is why our parents play the most crucial role in our development, with siblings an important second. However, schools could synergistically be vitally helpful in guiding this crucial process.

FAMILY FUNDAMENTALS FOR SUCCESS

It is crucial that parents and their families recognize that, first and foremost, their purpose is to prepare children for life.

So the first questions parents should ask themselves are: *Do our children recognize and believe this? Can they tell that our family is more important to us than our careers, marriage, or anything else in our lives? Do we have routines, traditions, outings, and special occasions that place family at the top of our priorities?*

Until the end of adolescence, parents assume ultimate responsibility for children's growth. But a profound measure of parental effectiveness is how well children assume the majority of this responsibility by age nineteen.

Since at birth the child has 0 percent of this responsibility, the parent's job is to instill at least 51 percent self-sufficiency in the child over those first nineteen years by utilizing chores and other responsibility measures.

The second job parents need to accomplish is helping the child realize his or her best, essential to the realization of fulfilling his or her unique potential and true destiny in life.

However, today many parents get sidetracked from fulfilling these two crucial responsibilities because of concerns of wanting to establish family relationships and "love."

What such parents fail to understand is that preparing children for life—helping them to become self-sufficient by age nineteen and to realize their best—by itself establishes a deep, loving relationship with children. Do this and your children will love and respect you for life.

I should also note that parents who become overly concerned about their children's behavior may be having difficulty because their concern is interfering with the normal growth of responsibility of their child.

However, at an often deep, unconscious level, children want and need the reassurance they are being well prepared for life in terms of their best and self-sufficiency. I had a strained relationship with my overly strict stepfather, but at a deeper level, I trusted his commitment to my growth, and I grew to love him for what he helped me do in life. On the surface we had nothing in common, but in life, I mirrored his character and sense of purpose—as did my older brother, Tom.

Since this deeper transformation provides the foundation for the development of our unique potential, the Unifying process is dedicated to strengthening and reaffirming the family cocoon. Family is the school's primary classroom and bellwether of the Unifying process. Family progress and excellence inevitably mean school progress and excellence.

This revolutionary educational approach leads Unifying parents to experience a major personal and parenting transformation. All family members are affected, including siblings who do not attend the school.

Given the power of family in human growth, parents hold the key that unlocks greatness. In a University of Chicago study of 120 exceptional individuals in the fields of science, mathematics, art, music, and athletics, the common thread researchers discovered in their greatness was "a long and intensive process of encouragement, nurturance, education, and training."[2] And parents always initiated this powerful growth process.

Since the Unifying process is dedicated to the development of our very best in search of our unique potential, this seminal study in the development of human excellence provides us with important guidance:

- On one hand, the study's reaffirmation of the dominant power of "encouragement, nurturance, education, and training" inspires Hyde's drive to help all students realize their deeper potentials. We know of no other school or program like the Unifying process that so comprehensively seeks this depth of personal growth excellence.
- On the other hand, the study's emphasis that this pursuit of excellence is "a long and intensive process" is sobering. It forces us to realize that this development of excellence (1) must begin well before the Unifying experience and (2) at a

depth at least compatible to the Unifying process; and further, that (3) it is unrealistic, even unwise and unfair, to expect students lacking this vital foundation to master Hyde-Bath in a limited two-, three- or even four-year period.

In the Hyde-Bath admission process, prospective parents and interviewers work closely together to determine whether the student has the necessary parent commitment to succeed at school. This in-depth assessment does more than predict the student's success at Hyde; it begins the development of an effective parent and family program to support the student's growth. Remember: in character development, parents are the primary teachers and the home the primary classroom.

The Unifying process itself has given us important clues of just what family resources are needed for success. These need to be continually recognized, supported, and strengthened during the Hyde experience. These fundamentals include:

1. Loyalty. Family is forever. Our spiritual family bonds, fused with our own personal commitments, determine the direction and nature of our lives. These spiritual bonds become part of our soul; families must fully respect family-of-origin bonds. But our family loyalties must always be directed to each member's best, not necessarily to what each may want from us. (For example, I learned how my misguided sense of loyalty to my wife, Blanche, helped enable her to avoid her deep need to confront her alcoholism.)

2. Purpose. Family is far more than deep human relationships; family prepares us to fulfill our character, unique potential, and destiny in life. Parents must continually model the pursuit of these deeper human potentials, which tells children we were not meant to live life on our terms, but rather to

seek to fulfill the larger purpose defined by our unique potential. This is the most crucial factor for success at school.

3. Respect. Until the end of adolescence, parents are primarily and crucially responsible for their children's future, so insubordination in any form must never be tolerated. Simply put, if children don't learn to fully respect their parents' guidance and direction, they will be unable to fully give and gain the respect of others in life. By the same token, parents must respect that raising children is the most important thing they will ever do in life, and their most powerful preparation comes from fulfilling their own unique destiny.

4. Character. The primary emphasis of family must always be character development. This becomes a compelling statement to children that they are meant to fulfill a larger purpose in life. Curiosity expands their horizons. Courage transcends their fears and complacency. Concern moves them beyond their inherent self-centeredness. Leadership draws out their unique potential. Integrity expresses their deeper selves. Parents must continually model these qualities to inspire their development in children.

5. Challenge. Every true leader has experienced at least one intense, transformational "crucible" experience, calling upon the adaptive capacity that allows them to *survive inevitable setbacks, heartbreaks, and difficulties, but also to learn from them.* The Unifying process is itself a crucible that best serves families whose challenges have taught their children the deeper value of resiliency—an essential quality for leadership. To face the inevitable crises of life, reliance upon character must almost become a reflexive action.

THE LETTING GO–TAKING HOLD PROCESS

Hyde parents need to learn to effectively apply the Letting Go–Taking Hold process in their child-rearing. They must continually determine where their own responsibility to their children's growth should end, and where their children's responsibility should begin. Many parents today are misguided in their efforts to help their children realize their true best, because they often assume responsibilities that should be the children's. Believe it or not, at a deeper level children have a real concern for their future, but this deeper responsibility in life scares them, so they feel relieved when parents continue to overprotect; this allows them to focus on the present and concerns like "What am I going to do Saturday night?"

In particular, many parents of off-track children unwittingly try to help and/or protect their children in a way that only encourages more off-track behavior from them.

Picture their off-track and growing children as being on an elevator going up, and each year they irresponsibly jump out a window, only to be caught by their desperate parents. As they reach more and more dangerous heights, the parents in panic finally yell up to their children they will no longer catch them, because the height may kill both of them. In the middle of all this, children simply jump, and parents instinctively try to catch them, regardless of what they have yelled.

So what can parents do to break this dangerous and destructive pattern?

Since they will always try to catch their child, the only solution is to not be there. Imagine the parent becoming distracted by someone in the distance, and so he or she leaves. Will the child still jump? Of course not; the child isn't stupid, just off-track.

The imagined distraction in the distance represents "taking hold." It means to start focusing on what parents can change—ourselves. The "letting go" is stopping our focus on the things we cannot change—our child's irresponsibility. Only our child can do that, no matter how difficult or scary change might be. And remember: our children are far more resourceful than we think they are.

Necessity is the mother of invention.

Once parents start to focus on their own growth, they begin to empower themselves to truly "take hold," that is, to exercise their true responsibilities in parenting, regardless of their children's behavior. If they really do, their children will begin to realize their own responsibilities in their growth.

Once parents correctly "take hold" of their responsibilities, they put themselves in a position to effectively motivate their children to effectively "take hold" of their responsibilities, although it may require an action they don't want to take—but need to.

It is crucially important that all the Unifying players—parents, students, teachers, and the community itself—clearly understand each other's roles and responsibilities, and help each other develop and sustain a strong and effective family-school cocoon. Character excellence requires both students and parents to maintain humility that keeps their power from interfering with the synergy of the cocoon.

So all should continually be sensitive to the hierarchy of authority in the Unifying cocoon. This is what it looks like:

- Highest level: The unique potential of the student is sacred. Student, parent, family, and school must always be willing to defer their own desires and authority in respect to the development of unique potential.

- Level 2: The student "owns" the unique potential, and, as the least mature player in the process, must continually be ready to defer to the help of others. Students will have ample opportunities to then step back and decide the value of that help.

- Level 3: The parent "owns" the family, and thus, as the dominant player in the process, must be continually ready to defer to the help of others in order to fully test the Unifying process in creating a more powerful family cocoon. Parents will have ample opportunities to step back and decide the value of that help.

- Level 4: The teacher "owns" the school Unifying process, and thus must ensure that the efforts of the student, parents, and other community members continually respect the unique potential and growth needs of the student.

- Level 5: All members of the Unifying community are responsible for continually giving their honest and best perceptions of the efforts of the student, parent, family, teacher, school, and community itself.

There may be serious consequences in life when this hierarchy of authority in the Unifying cocoon is not fully respected. For example, concerned parents—the most influential Hyde figures—may naturally try to sway the process in directions they feel are better for their children's future.

This unwittingly defeats the purpose of the Hyde cocoon, which is to force students to learn to fully rely upon their own character in facing the challenges of life. Children may unconsciously continue to some degree to rely upon such parental "help." But in life, they will have only their character, not their parents. This is a far more serious problem than parents today realize.

THE SPIRITUAL PARENT

Raising children is the biggest job we will ever have. It is also the most difficult. But doing it right is the ultimate human fulfillment, and transforms a parent's life as well as a child's.

The pursuit of our own unique destiny is our most powerful parenting tool. It provides the vital inspiration for our children to pursue their own unique potential, and forces us to model our very best for them—just what they need to fulfill their own destiny.

It takes discipline to ensure that our parenting always takes priority over our other challenges, issues, and problems—in marriage, career, and personal life. Given the power parents have over children, parenting also takes a higher level of humility than we have ever known. Kahlil Gibran profoundly describes this humility in "On Children" from *The Prophet*.

Parenting and teaching have taught me the deepest reverence for Gibran's wisdom. Children begin life totally dependent upon us, but Gibran reminds us that as parents we are merely assistants to a power greater than ourselves. We must resist raising children in our own image, for the purpose of their lives is beyond our comprehension.

This can be an ego-deflating realization for dedicated parents, but it is also liberating. It means we are not ultimately responsible for our children's destinies; all we are required to do is our best. And whatever our parenting problems, help will always be available from this greater power that loves us as "the bow that is stable."

This leads to the definition of a spiritual parent: one who humbly accepts that his or her child has a purpose and a destiny dictated by a higher power. This belief is essential to helping our children realize their inner greatness. Let me illustrate.

Suppose your fifteen-year-old son skins his knee, and with time the wound unaccountably becomes worse. The doctor, after extensive treatment, finds that the wound has gangrene and reluctantly recommends amputation. You call in a specialist from another city, who confirms the tragic diagnosis. You finally muster the courage to tell your son that he must have the operation because the alternative is death. He refuses, saying, "I'd rather be dead than crippled and unable to play ball." What do you do?

In fact, this scenario is based on a true account in the life of Dwight Eisenhower. At age fifteen, Ike was faced with such a life-threatening wound and argued against amputation so that he could continue to play football.

Although his parents were against contact sports, they acknowledged their son's right to make such a decision and sorrowfully accepted his choice. Obviously, his decision turned out to be right, as he made a miraculous recovery.

When I first read Ike's account of this episode, I was curious to see how my wife, Blanche, would react, because I considered her to be a spiritual parent. I asked what she would do if the same thing were to happen to our son Malcolm at age fifteen, and I got this exchange.

"I would check with other doctors," she replied.

"Suppose they agreed?"

"Well . . . then I would talk to Malcolm."

"But suppose he still balked?"

"Well . . . we'd talk some more."

"Blanche, I know you're confident that you could eventually bring Malcolm around, but suppose you couldn't?"

After a long pause she said, "It would kill me, but I guess I would have to go along with his refusal."

I expected this answer from Blanche, who ultimately accepted that such a decision would be between her fifteen-year-old son and his god. However, I know of few parents who could so decide. The vast majority of American parents today are not spiritually prepared to make such a decision.

Most would have saved Ike's life but not his leg—or his dreams. His life would have headed in a different direction.

It is the creative potential itself in human beings that is the image of God. —Mary Daly

I have related this situation to a number of parents and asked how they would react. Virtually all of them said they would reluctantly tell the doctors to amputate.

And most are probably correct in doing so. Most American parents simply have not prepared their teenagers to accept a deeper responsibility for their lives, and so if they refused the amputation, parents would not be able to trust that their teenager recognized the deeper realities of the situation. Thus, parents would feel compelled to make the decision themselves, which in the vast majority of cases is what their teenager wants them to do.

Clearly the Eisenhowers had so prepared Ike. Even though Ike said he refused the amputation so he could play ball, my understanding of unique potential says that even at fifteen, his deeper vision of his future told him he needed that leg. So at that crucial moment of truth, he was guided not by his parents but by his conscience—the compass of his destiny.

It is no coincidence that both Blanche's parents and Dwight Eisenhower's lived on a farm. This farm upbringing no doubt instilled in them a deep humility and respect for a power and purpose beyond themselves.

Perhaps because farmers recognize that their livelihood is totally dependent upon nature, over which they have no control, they more easily accept that neither can they control the growth of their children. Just as nature rules the farm, destiny dictates the proper development of a child's uniqueness.

Few parents will ever have to face such a life-threatening situation. But if we hope to inspire greatness in our children, we must learn to discipline our parent-child relationships, to continually turn over responsibilities to our growing children. It leads our children to listen to their deeper selves and be guided by their conscience. I credit my parents' discipline in this regard (except for their alcoholism) for the strong relationship I have developed in life with my conscience, which has led me to a wonderful life I never could have imagined.

Just as we are gifted with a unique potential, so are we endowed with deeper child-rearing instincts. But we must be able to transcend our deepest emotions to realize those instincts.

A mama bear could teach us how to raise children. She gradually teaches her cub how to hunt for itself. When the cub makes mistakes, like attacking a porcupine, she does not step in. This is a vital part of the cub's education.

After a year, she turns on her cub, chasing it up a tree. Then she walks away, never to see her cub again. Her act kills her cub's dependence on her, making him doubt he ever again wants to find this mother turned monster.

Now the cub begins to fully rely on his own potentials to live.

We humans have those parenting instincts, but we often allow our personal issues and desires to interfere with them. Our dedication to the Unifying process not only enables us to develop our own unique potential, but also empowers our deeper child-rearing instincts.

Our parenting also needs the serenity prayer:

God grant me the serenity to accept the things I cannot change,
The courage to change the things I can,
And the wisdom to know the difference.

The serenity prayer provides parents with an excellent discipline to keep their efforts focused on their own responsibilities, thus almost compelling their children to address theirs.

PRINCIPLES, NOT PERSONALITIES, RAISE CHILDREN

We ourselves are imperfect; so it is vital that our principles always take precedence in our parenting. In chapter 3, I told the story about how Malcolm, at age three, corrected my behavior. It illustrated how early children learn our family principles.

To reemphasize some points I made earlier:

Parents are the most powerful authority in children's lives. Since we cannot abdicate this authority, it becomes vital to teach our kids that our principles and not we ourselves are the ultimate authority. Making principles the final authority avoids unnecessary power struggles with growing children.

Kids are constantly testing limits to determine their capabilities; they will inevitably test parents who impose those limits. Even the best of us will sometimes be inconsistent or wrong, which invites any kid to challenge parental boundaries. But principles will be the same tomorrow as they are today, leaving kids to question parental interpretation of principles, not parents themselves. This allows kids to accept parental authority without feeling they are just giving in.

Emphasizing principles is also an effective way to make children responsible for their own growth. If we parent "out of our heads," the burden is on us to create rules our children can follow. But principles shift this responsibility to kids, who learn to interpret the principles in order to determine for themselves what actions may be right or acceptable in various situations.

The leadership of principles practically forces us to raise children effectively. The only true way we teach children is by example. Principles make us practice what we preach, and therefore become the means for kids to understand our actions in a deeper way.

A lack of discipline permeates American parenting today. Since parents have a confused idea of just where their own efforts fit into a larger process, they pass on this confusion to their children.

Parents must help their children learn how to determine the difference between their growth *needs*, what they must gain to become the great individuals they were meant to be, and their *wants*, what they desire that may sometimes hinder their best growth.

Because of the limitations parents experience in our own upbringing, we are increasingly entering parenthood with some need-versus-want confusion within ourselves. Since the same is true for our spouses, our marriages may get tangled in unproductive wants, thus establishing a shaky foundation for our child-rearing. Without clearly understanding their own deeper growth needs, children may end up in power struggles with us and/or each other, which they will unwittingly reproduce someday in their own parenting.

Principles provide a vital discipline to help us separate our own wants and needs, thus allowing us to model character and unique potential growth for our children. This discipline is then much more easily accepted by our children.

PARENTING WITH THE UNIFYING FIVE WORDS AND FIVE PRINCIPLES

We encourage families to develop principles that express their family's uniqueness. But we also strongly urge them to adopt and practice the Unifying Five Words and Five Principles.

Here is how the Five Principles relate to family dynamics:

- Destiny: *Each of us is gifted with a unique potential that defines a destiny.* Destiny is a constant reminder that each of us has a larger purpose in life to fulfill, which keeps the emphasis on doing our best, and avoids the numbness of complacency. Destiny reaffirms the deeper respect family members must maintain for each other. It forces us to address our prejudices by accepting that everyone has a unique destiny as important as our own.

A Parent Challenges the Hyde High Ropes Course. *Hyde School*

- Humility: *We trust in a power and a purpose beyond ourselves.* The Humility principle provides us with a vital check on our egos and encourages us to accept direction from family members and others. At a deeper level, humility develops our faith in a higher power and in ourselves. Becoming an effective parent requires rigorously addressing one's own beliefs.

- Conscience: *We achieve our best through character and conscience.* The Conscience principle sets the highest family standard for one's best. It compels family members to value right and wrong, and to accept that their actions reflect their character. The socks story revealed Malcolm's ability at age three to value his own sense of right and wrong more than his reverence for his parents. Clearly this path will help children morally transcend peer pressure and other outside influences, and ultimately listen to and act upon their conscience—the compass of one's destiny.

- Truth: *Truth is our primary guide.* Accepting truth as the ultimate authority in the family keeps personalities, relationships, and other dynamics from distracting the family from its basic purpose. Also, maintaining family devotion to truth becomes a powerful gift to children to effectively deal with their lives.

- Brother's/Sister's Keeper: *We help others achieve their best.* Respecting Brother's/Sister's Keeper in family relationships is a vital way to reaffirm the deeper purpose of the family, to maintain its commitment to truth, and to help all family members realize their best. The Keeper principle prepares children to develop strong relationships in their lives, to continually gain the power of synergy, and to help others as they have been helped.

The Five Principles are "we" concepts. They primarily deal with our relationships with others. The Five Words are "I" concepts. They primarily deal with our own growth and development.
Here is how the Five Words relate to family dynamics:

- Curiosity: *I am a learner.* Curiosity helps to develop the family as a learning unit, and begins the process of teaching children self-discipline and responsibility for their own growth. Parents should initiate and inspire children's curiosity, with reading in particular. Parents should expose children to new interests while supporting their longtime interests. Exploration needs to be valued; the biggest enemy of unique potential is complacency.

- Courage: *I learn the most about myself by accepting challenges.* Courage is the foundation of individuality and self-confidence. The need for courage resonates with children. The enduring popularity of the 1939 movie *The Wizard of Oz* speaks to the story's modern metaphor for character development and unique potential. All children can identify with Cowardly Lion. Children need challenges—facing physical pain or a bully, standing up to peer pressure or a fear, not quitting when something difficult occurs are all examples. Children need chores and even some elements of a Marine boot camp. Shoddy efforts must be challenged. Alert parents watch for crucial moments of courage, confirm their importance, don't let children off the hook, and celebrate their children's personal triumphs.

- Concern: *I need a challenging and supportive community to develop my character.* Children begin to develop their sensitivity, compassion, and empathy in their family. They learn to appreciate the concerns of other family members. While they are usually on the receiving end of concern, children also learn to be sensitive to the needs of others, and at least express concern for others at a Motions level. In time, this Motions level of concern will grow into a more meaningful level of growth we call synergy (1 + 1 = 3), and eventually all family members, having internalized synergy, will naturally help one another in any situation.

- Leadership: *I am a leader by asking the best of myself and others.* Establishing Brother's/Sister's Keeper in the family virtually guarantees the development of children's leadership potential. As they experience the Effort and Excellence stages of concern, they begin to appreciate how others demanding their best have guided them through their own Motions learning. This realization makes them feel almost compelled to help others as they have been helped—the key to their leadership. Leadership leads kids to draw upon deeper potentials that relate more to their larger purpose in life. It empowers them to move beyond their earlier center-of-the-universe narcissism and gain confidence and fulfillment in their abilities to help others. In essence, they begin to see themselves in a larger light.

- Integrity: *I am gifted with a unique potential, and conscience is my guide in discovering it.* Just as courage develops our individuality, integrity leads us on the path to discover our unique potential. But integrity is a difficult character quality for kids to internalize and trust. They don't yet know who they are, and being honest sometimes doesn't seem to them to work out very well. So they become vulnerable and susceptible to the glamour of images as well as the pressure of peers and commercial interests. As in the development of all qualities of character, kids are best taught integrity by parents and teachers who have the confidence and courage to be themselves, "warts and all," in all situations and with all people. Parents must be vigilant in encouraging children's growth more than their achievements, particularly when they have the courage to truly be themselves. Once kids fully enter Motions learning in integrity, they become aware of a deeper respect they gain from themselves and others, which motivates them into the Effort stage. In time they will gain the confidence to address their "moments of truth" in life by first listening to their own sense of right and wrong—the key to allowing conscience to guide their lives.

A HYDE PARENT WRITES ABOUT PERSONAL STRUGGLES

Dear Joe:

We started Hyde four months ago. You came over to us in the dining room that dreary dark day when we were dropping Will off, and introduced yourself with a big smile on your face. I remember thinking, how can he be so cheerful at a time like this? To be honest, we didn't know what we were getting into and we were uncertain. But driving back home from Family Weekend last Sunday, I sang at the top of my lungs in the car, as I thought of what had happened since then:

In January, Will was angry, disrespectful, monosyllabic, and without hope. He's now affectionate, open, and trying things that are hard for him. He is articulate, he smiles, and he pushes himself to do things that he's afraid of failing, like talking in seminars and trying out for (and making) varsity lacrosse. He still struggles in many areas, but what he has learned is that he doesn't have to be perfect the first time, or all the time; that there is a way of learning from not being perfect always and moving on. He is able to talk unguardedly about his fears and hopes. He's worried about where he is academically, but at least he is worried, and he's committed to coming to Hyde next year. He says to his friends back home: "I don't like it, but it is the best thing that ever happened to me."

Since January, I myself have:

- *Gained a whole new family made up of dozens of parents, kids, and faculty, with whom I have explored feelings that I never told to anyone, ever;*
- *Learned how my fear of taking risks and letting my guard down is a behavior I've taught to Will. I see it in him and I now understand it, for the first time. Talking about those feelings in front of Will has helped him see himself in a new light;*
- *Sung a solo in front of a lot of people, including my son, who had a big smile on his face hearing me;*
- *Danced a complicated (for me) routine in front of hundreds of people last weekend;*
- *Begun to be able to talk in front of a group—something I've successfully avoided all my life—especially about private feelings;*
- *Done water-coloring and line drawings again, after having dropped it for years, thinking I needed to spend time working and being a mother. I didn't know, until we started at Hyde, how important it is to Will (and to me) that I pursue my own potential.*

We still have a long way to go, but I feel complete confidence in the process for the journey.

THE TEN UNIFYING PRIORITIES

Unifying parent and student responsibilities have been outlined. Other family members are urged to respect and practice these responsibilities as well. The entire family is expected to practice the ten priorities as outlined in the book *The Biggest Job We'll Ever Have*, by Malcolm and Laura Gauld. These priorities form the foundation of the family program at Hyde, and prepare both parents and children for the Unifying experience. These are the priorities:

1. Truth over harmony. The first and foremost responsibility of family is to properly prepare children for life. Always placing truth above harmony in family values reaffirms this responsibility, and helps the family become the powerful cocoon that nature has intended it to be.

2. Principles over rules. Always placing principles above rules reaffirms the family's basic purpose, and further ensures that the family is dominated by its principles, not by its personalities.

3. Attitude over aptitude. The emphasis on respecting positive and productive attitudes reaffirms the development of character in the family, and counteracts the present and unhealthy emphasis in our society on aptitude, talent, and ability. We are in life whatever our unique potential guides us to be.

4. Set high expectations and let go of the outcome. High expectations are essential to the full development of our unique potential. By letting go of the outcome of these expectations, we ensure that we are not undermined by an emphasis on result instead of growth.

5. Value success and failure. Our courage in pursuing our high expectations will inevitably lead to both success and failure. By valuing both, we gain confidence from our successes, but we often learn the most from our failures.

6. Allow obstacles to become opportunities. We were meant to be challenged by life in order to fully realize our unique potential and our destiny. We must learn to accept that our obstacles in life are there for a purpose; thus, they become opportunities to help us discover both ourselves and our purpose in life. (*I thank God for my handicaps, for through them, I have found myself, my work, and my God.* —Helen Keller)

7. Take hold and let go. We may not be able to change others in our family, but we can always change ourselves. By letting go of the things we cannot change (others) and taking hold of the things we can (ourselves), we inspire others to follow our lead.

8. Create a character culture. By emphasizing the development of character in our family and our home, we create the cocoon that will enable our children and ourselves to transcend from our lesser selves to our higher human selves.

9. Have the humility to ask for and accept help. Others can see our unique potential and our best in ways we cannot. By asking for and receiving help, we begin to experience a synergy that enables us to reach a higher best in ourselves, and empowers us to help others.

10. Inspiration: Job #1. Character is primarily taught by example. By dedicating ourselves to develop the character necessary to realize our unique potential, we provide the inspiration and the most powerful means to help other family members follow our lead.

The development of the family is the most powerful part of the Unifying process. Our Hyde-Bath Graduation Morning Breakfast ceremony marks the graduation of senior parents. It is a deeply moving experience; each parent receives a diploma after the reading of a message from their senior student.

Some examples of these words from seniors to their parents:

Dad, the past four years of getting to know you have been a joy. I commend you for the strength you showed when I came to Hyde and begged you to take me home, and the courage to take the challenge of learning about yourself and then bettering yourself. You make me want to be a better person.

Mom, when you conquered the ropes course you inspired me. You are willing to continually challenge yourself in the desire to learn more about yourself. It demonstrates to me how I want to live my life: be curious, face fears, and be courageous.

Dad, for so long your touch felt like daggers and from each other misery and defeat rained down on us. Our rebirth came with sacrifice, forgiveness, and thousands of tears. It was your relentless search for your soul instead of saving mine that has allowed us to love again. You are the strongest, softest man I know.

Mom, your willingness to totally commit yourself to this place and me over the last three years is amazing. You inspire me through your passions; never stop writing your poetry—I believe that is what will set you free.

Dad, who would've thought? My dad working on Habitat, doing the ropes course, confronting co-workers, learning guitar . . . Through embracing your passions and your fears, you have shown me it is never too late to face mine. More impor-

tantly, you have modeled what it means to be a man of integrity, of honor, and above all, a gentleman.

Mom, three years ago when we first came to Hyde, you were asked by the interviewer, "What do you need to work on in yourself?" and you sat there speechless. Through the years of pushing through confrontations, mandatory fun, midnight joyrides, and Family Weekends, our trust in each other has grown and will keep on growing with the same continual efforts. Your courage to confront your fears, first on the ropes course, then on the dance floor, and finally on the wilderness FLC, served as a source of inspiration and an example of risk-taking for me.

I once counted the key words seniors used in writing about their parents. The word "love" was highly prevalent, but the single word almost every senior used was "inspire." When the Unifying process is working on all cylinders, what happens at Hyde simply supports how parents are raising their children.

NOTES

1. Encyclopedia.com, "Coleman Report," March 5, 2021, https://www.encyclopedia.com/social-sciences/dictionaries-thesauruses-pictures-and-press-releases/coleman-report.

2. Benjamin S. Bloom, ed., *Developing Talent in Young People* (New York: Ballantine, 1985).

10

THE UNIFYING INNER LEADERSHIP MODEL

Five Deliverables

Traditional education is focused on achievement and what we can do. However, Unifying education is focused on the development of our unique potential and thus first focused on who we are and our character development. Unifying's Inner Leadership Model is an approach to developing leadership from the inside out. The five deliverables of the program are self-awareness, public speaking confidence, uncomfortable challenges, meaningful relationships, and family context.

SELF-AWARENESS

Aristotle said, "Educating the mind without educating the heart is no education at all." The development of unique potential begins with self-awareness, which, as Aristotle noted, centers education not on the mind, but more deeply on the heart, giving life to phrases like "trust your heart," "speak from your heart," and "follow your heart."

However, just as we rigorously develop our mind, so must we rigorously develop our heart. We need to recognize that as we grow, we will have many unproductive feelings—for example, hate, fear, anger, instant gratification—that may seem "heartfelt," but are really counter to the development of our character and unique potential. So we need to develop a discipline and structure that will carefully distinguish and address the emotions that develop our heart and mind to express the best in ourselves in order to fulfill our destiny.

Who am I? This question begins the Hyde process. Addressing the three critical questions—*Who am I? Where am I going? What do I need to get there?*—helps guide us on the path of our destiny.

Think back to your childhood and your life to try to determine these:

- Vision: Try to remember the visions you have had for your life, beginning with your early childhood. Are there some that particularly stand out to you?
- Strengths: Identify your strengths, the qualities you have expressed, or potentials you believe you have yet to fully express. Is there anything else that may give you confidence?
- Challenges: Identify those experiences—and even thoughts, feelings, and attitudes—that have held you back from being your best. Is anything else in your way?

As we determine our vision, strengths, and challenges, we gain a much clearer sense of who we are and where we are going, and we are better able to determine how we are going to get there.

Assessing Emotional Intelligence

Self-awareness gives us the ability to recognize and understand personal moods, emotions, and drives, as well as their effect on others. Given that we are imperfect, we need to readily be open to assessing the negative side of ourselves, even with a sense of humor. Often, our emotions appear out of thin air, so it is good practice to try to figure out where these emotions come from and why they are there.

What This Wrestler Learns about Himself Transcends Winning or Losing.
Hyde School

Self-management gives us the control to act and express ourselves the way we wish to. We've all had situations in life where our emotions usurped our better judgment. Self-management brings our ability to think before acting together with our disruptive impulses and moods. But on a larger scale, we are coordinating our mind, heart, and soul potentials.

Social awareness gives us the ability to understand other people and their emotions. Regardless of the culture, the three things to study are emotions, facial expressions, and body language. And to really learn, we must become much more listeners than talkers. Those who seriously study people often come to deeply understand them, even to "read" their actions.

Social management gives us the ability to manage relationships. Self-awareness helps us note our feelings and judge whether our needs are being met, self-management helps us express our feelings effectively, and social awareness helps us understand the needs and feelings of others. So we are well equipped to develop effective relationships that will greatly improve our organization. As I said early in this book, it highlights the sense of "belonging"— what makes groups or organizations highly successful.

The diagram on the next page (from *Emotional Intelligence 2.0* by Travis Bradberry and Jean Greaves) illustrates how the thoughtful development of self-awareness creates a chain reaction that leads to both self-management and social awareness, and ultimately to relationship management.

Discovery Group Curriculum

The Unifying Discovery Group connects a small group of students to a teacher, who meet weekly. The basic purpose is to keep the educational focus on the individual student, emphasizing the development of unique potential and character, while addressing

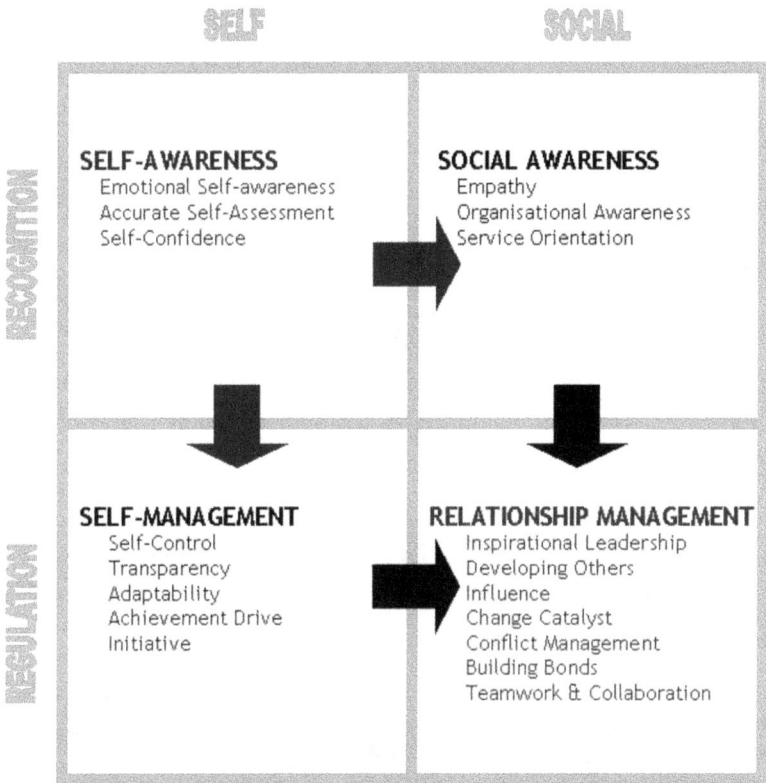

The Development of Self-awareness. Emotional Intelligence 2.0 *by Travis Bradbury and Jean Greaves*

attitudes, effort, strengths, and challenges, reflected both at school and at home.

The group provides synergistic power to the student, including Brother's/Sister's Keeper relationships that challenge and support each one's best. In addition, the close leader relationship helps both faculty and community remain sensitive to each student's situation and best, and seeks to involve the student's parents and family in the self-discovery process.

Some public schools have adapted the Unifying Discovery Group concept, using homerooms made up of mixed-grade students, who weekly have athletic, performing arts, community service, school jobs, and seminars. One school system has had this program for twenty-five years.

PUBLIC SPEAKING CONFIDENCE

If we give a great speech but nobody can hear us, what is its value? Before our message can transform our audience, we need to develop our potentials for being heard, which means being able to raise our volume to comfortably reach the most distant listener. Also, the effectiveness of our speech is directly tied to our body language, which conveys our passion and/or conviction in what we are talking about. It is said that an audience generally decides in

Hyde Graduating Seniors Speak for 1–2 Minutes. *Hyde School*

the first ten seconds if a speaker has a speech of value, which makes our body language the deciding factor.

One of the great human fears is public speaking. We believe this fear is rooted in our schooling, where we are essentially trained to be passive listeners to (not professors of) knowledge. But view us on the playground, and you see us with a very different persona and voice (*"HEY! COME ON OVER HERE!"*), one alive in heart, body, and soul.

This transformation is at the heart of the Hyde public speaking course—helping students have the courage to be their playground selves and become more of this persona both in life and in school, including the classroom. While they will need to learn some important new skills to assist them in this public transformation, their playground experience already gives them the potentials required to make them effective, even outstanding speakers.

The benefits are enormous. For once we become comfortable and effective talking to larger groups, we find ourselves really being able to connect to smaller groups and to others in our personal relationships. The process helps bring out a deeper part of ourselves that makes us more real, interesting, sensitive, and attractive to others. We then begin to connect to others in creating the powerful synergy that enables us and them to realize higher personal bests beyond our own efforts: synergy, or $1 + 1 = 3$.

But perhaps the greatest value of becoming our playground selves in public speaking is in changing our passive school persona to an assertive personality. This enables us to utilize our unique potential and become more successful in life.

At Hyde-Bath, we help the entire school do exercises that emphasize the playground voice and actions. Seniors take the Hyde School public speaking course, ultimately serving as both models and assistants in helping the student body develop public speaking skills and confidence.

Formal and Informal Speaking

There are many opportunities where students are encouraged to speak informally: in class, in community and school meetings, and in the family program. It is expected to be a natural expression of their inner leadership. In addition, there are more formal times when students are asked to take leadership roles in class or in community and school meetings and in the parent and family program. Sometimes students will tell their personal stories in school meetings; students also host prospective families and other guests.

It is a Hyde tradition that seniors speak at graduation, summarizing in one to two minutes what they have learned from life and their Hyde education. It is often said that a Hyde education begins with an interview and ends in a speech.

TACKLING CHALLENGES OUTSIDE OUR COMFORT ZONE

The first critical step in realizing both our unique potential and our inner leadership is developing mastery over our attitudes and effort in order to be able to effectively express our hearts and minds and be our best selves.

Mastery of Structure and Discipline

These two reflections from students demonstrate the impact of accepting challenges outside our comfort zone and mastery over discipline.

> *One of my defining moments was about my courage and how I tend to fly under the radar at Hyde. My Discovery Group leader challenged me to play my harmonica at the coffeehouse.*

An Emotional Moment at a Hyde Graduation. *Hyde School*

At first I was nervous and I procrastinated, not even practic-
ing. Finally, I pulled one of my friends aside to play guitar and
we wrote a quick song. I was so nervous getting up on the stage,
but we played anyway and it was great. Now I fully intend to
play at every coffeehouse.

On my wrestling team every day, whether practices, matches,
or tournaments, I experience Rigor, Brother's Keeper, and
"Never Lie–Never Quit." Every day in the wrestling room with
the extreme amounts of Brother's Keeper displayed, there is no
room for me not to do my best. In the end, it all ties together; I
know all the hard work pays off.

We can be held back by self-serving emotions and motivations that
prompt us to act on the basis of our likes and dislikes, desires and
fears. These keep us from realizing our powerful self-transcending
emotions and motivations that prompt us to go beyond ourselves

and seek what is truly worthwhile in life: truth, beauty, excellence, noble deeds, respect for individual persons, love, destiny.

As we become able to thrive in the structure of the Unifying experience with self-discipline and resilience, we establish a vital foundation for our future growth at school and in life:

- We have essentially learned how to put our character in charge of counter attitudes, emotions, and motivations that take us away from our best self, while emphasizing the positive ones that encourage a deeper development of our conscience and unique potential.

- Our work on discipline and structure is developing our inner leadership, and we are gaining trust in the community by demonstrating that we can be a good follower—the first step to being trusted as a leader.

Leadership Opportunities

The Unifying program and process have evolved over the past fifty years, with the primary goal of developing unique potential with an emphasis on the Five Words and Five Principles, while maintaining a college preparatory curriculum. Sports, dorms, and jobs were part of the program from the beginning, along with early signs of community service.

Parents and family became part of the program in 1974, with performing arts skyrocketing in 1976 on the great success of Hyde's *America's Spirit* show that toured the Eastern Seaboard, including the Kennedy Center and Broadway. It was also funded by the government to perform for Job Corps sites, remaining a hit until 1984.

Further, students began effectively pursuing leadership opportunities—whether in school, like conducting an admissions tour, or outside, like joining a Habitat for Humanity project—seeking to challenge themselves. Students also express leadership in our parent/family program.

Challenges Unique to Each Student

No matter how challenging the Hyde program, our unique potential and our unique selves have had singular experiences in life. So if we take our background as a whole, there exists a unique challenge for us that, if met, would have great meaning for both ourselves and our unique potential.

But finding that unique challenge may be difficult. Is it related to our greatest fear? Is it buried in our subconscious—something we want to forget? It probably requires us to go deeper into ourselves than we want to go. After I founded Hyde School to explore the development of unique potential and character, I knew I had to challenge my fear of heights—something I had always known and tried to ignore.

The challenge we need may deal with our childhood years. I have often said that all of us have childhood issues that, left unaddressed, hold us back in life. At age eighty, I attended the Hoffman Institute and dealt with attitudes of anger, frustration, impatience, and sarcasm, all rooted in my childhood experience. After addressing these issues, I was able to shed their hold on me. I just wish I had done it sooner in my life.

MEANINGFUL RELATIONSHIPS

The reason our species survived where others like Neanderthals did not is the fact we humans depended upon each other for strength from our beginnings. Empathy is now so deep in our DNA that studies show isolation leads to a shorter life.[1]

So we need to both renew and expand our relationships to lead healthy and longer lives.

Expanding Contacts and Difficult Conversations

If we remain neutral, then we have only those we accept and know and those we don't. That's a recipe for separation, mistrust, and even eventual conflict—as we've seen globally. But if we consistently seek to both strengthen and widen our relationships, as challenging as they might be, they become a powerful source of growth for us, deepening our outlook and insight, while giving us a greater sense of confidence and maturity.

It takes trust to make relationships meaningful and long lasting, which requires truth over harmony. In order to maintain this truth priority, we must not avoid difficult conversations. Relationships built on common interests or mutual benefits may not last, but relationships with people in our lives whose character and words we trust do last.

Once we have the courage—and the curiosity—to begin to practice truth over harmony in our relationships, we begin to appreciate the trust, plus the deeper understanding and respect for others it brings, as well as feel serenity and self-confidence. That is the recipe for building meaningful relationships.

Brother's/Sister's Keeper

Now we may feel the desire to share these deeper feelings with those who felt the same way we did when our relationships were harmony over truth. We begin to see Brother's/Sister's Keeper—

We help others achieve their best—in a different light. We feel the urge to help other people experience what we have experienced.

However, remembering our old attitudes, we know this won't be easy. In essence, we will have to challenge attitudes we completely understand, and learn to trust that our concern and empathy will help others as we were helped.

We all know we need to do our best to be successful and fulfilled in life. Imagine the depth of friendship accomplished when you know your friend is absolutely committed to the truth and helping you do your best. That is why it is called Brother's/ Sister's Keeper.

One Hyde student shares his motivation to change:

> *A particular example of Brother's Keeper changed my attitude. I was not close to going after my best and I didn't care. Then a good friend told me he was going to make a change in his life and he wanted me to do it with him. This meant a lot to me because we were getting into lots of trouble together. His genuine concern made me decide to get honest and make a step toward going after my best. It was a defining moment for me at Hyde.*

Concern Meetings

There are times when the best efforts of concerned students and teachers have minimal success in helping a student experience the transformational Brother's/Sister's Keeper process. What can prove to be helpful at such times is to call a "concern meeting" for the student, where students and faculty are invited to meet with the student to try to create a synergistic experience that pulls together many interactions with the student. The power of this experience can often bring new insights to the student regarding his or her growth.

FAMILY CONTEXT

While our family program was developed in an independent boarding school, much of it has been replicated in our Hyde charter schools. Also, the Unifying Discovery Group program provides an opportunity to connect schoolwork with families.

Addressing Childhood Experiences

From the instant we are born, we imitate those who raise us. In terms of our values, character, and sense of purpose and right and wrong, these imitations become some of our greatest strengths. However, since all of us are imperfect, both our parents/guardians and ourselves also imitated the shortcomings of those who raised us in our childhoods. Unaddressed, these negative emotional dispositions (NEDs) become deeply embedded in us, and they be-

A Family Works on Journaling Questions during Parents Weekend. *Hyde School*

come challenges we need to address in order to develop our best and our unique potential.

Childhood Spirit

As we review our attitudes, behaviors, and childhood experiences to identify these NEDs, the work should put us back in touch with our childhood spirit, which can be blocked by NEDs and other childhood experiences.

Childhood spirit is our natural connection to our unique potential, and needs to be integrated into our identity in order to live a truly fulfilling and meaningful life. So appreciate all the wonderful strengths—character, values, sense of purpose—you imitated from those who raised you, but also recognize and address the NEDs you imitated that undermine your unique potential. This is a critical step in releasing your childhood spirit.

Family Learning Center, Family Days, and Family Weekends

A major part of the Hyde-Bath program occurs when parents come to the campus so they can participate as families in the Hyde process. This helps fulfill the teaching tenet: in character development, parents are the primary teachers and home the primary classroom.

Both student and parent address their own growth as well as their roles in order to bond and make the family work more effectively. The synergy that is created by bringing Unifying families together with teachers to do this work is powerful.

Remember, both student and parent have the opportunity to visit their childhoods in these sessions. And childhood is the source of our dreams that may express our unique potential and also the source of the NEDs both parents and children imitated in their adolescence.

Hyde public charter schools use a Family Day program in fall and spring to bring students and parents/guardians together for the same purpose. Seminars and other sharing activities give the community a common experience with the Unifying process.

Taking Hold and Letting Go

As students begin the teen years, both they and their parents begin the final letting-go process that hopefully prepares students to begin to assume the responsibility of self-sufficiency when they enter their twenties.

This teen period for parents is one of constant decisions about what student responsibilities to let go of and thus what students need to take hold of, and how to handle accountability. For example, many parents so strongly want to ensure that their child goes to college, they are unwilling to give up that responsibility to their child.

Such parents will probably get their child into some college, but the child won't last long. Students who handle college well have achieved a level of self-sufficiency that enables them to recognize and meet challenges like living and learning independently.

Parents should help their child develop that level of self-sufficiency well before college, even if it means first testing life on one's own after high school graduation to find it. I know it would have made a big difference in my own college career.

As we review the five deliverables—self-awareness, public speaking confidence, uncomfortable challenges, meaningful relationships, family context—we realize that not only is the student being prepared to be a leader, but the deliverables also deepen the development of unique potential and individual strengths.

NOTE

1. Jessica Firger, "Too Much 'Alone Time' May Shorten Your Life," March 13, 2015, https://www.cbsnews.com/news/social-isolation-loneliness-may-shorten-your-life.

INDEX

academics: character development focus, 151; concerns and dissatisfaction with, 147–151; cultural pecking order in, xviii; fundamentals for intellectual character, 156–158; grading systems, 152; pathway to excellence, 167–169; purpose of, 152–156; transformation needed in, 150–151. *See also* AICR academic practices

ACEs (adverse childhood experiences), 95

achievement grades, 152

Action-Reflection Learning Cycle: ancient proverb describing, 109–110; cocoon analogy, 110–113; developing an identity through, 84; ego and, 92; golf analogy, 84, 109; integration of thoughts and actions, 114–117; internalization of thoughts and actions, 117–118; traditional education comparison, 113–114. *See also* academics; Unifying seminars

adverse childhood experiences (ACEs), 95

AICR academic practices: attentiveness, 158–160; critical thinking, 162–164; insightfulness, 160–162; responsibility, 36, 164–167

alcoholism, experiences with, 94–95, 141–142

alumni parents, 49

amputation story, 182–185

Anda, Robert, 95

Aristotle, 112, 199

the arts, 156

attentiveness, 158–160

attitude of students, 194

authority: head of school, 45, 47; hierarchy of, 180–181; principles as, 37–38, 186–187

bear cubs and mama bear, 185

The Biggest Job We'll Ever Have (Gauld), 194–195

Billings, Josh, 96

board of governors, 49

body language, 205

Born to Win, Schooled to Lose (Georgetown University study), xviii

Bradberry, Travis, 202

Brooks, Garth, 96
Brother's/Sister's Keepers: in family
    relationships, 189, 191; students as
    teachers, 60–61; as
    transformational, 210–211; as
    Unifying principle, 26, 32–34
bullying, xviii

Campbell, Joseph, 4
Carrel, Alexis, 13
challenges: in Hyde School
    Community, 7, 114–117; outside
    our comfort zone, 206–209; as
    transformational experiences, 16,
    178; types of, 117; unique potential
    and, 209
character: cautionary note, 15–16;
    defined, 14–15; as destiny, 11–12;
    developing, 18–19, 27, 48–51,
    113–114, 131–132, 151; intellectual
    character, 100, 156–158; journaling
    to discover, 19–23; moral character,
    156–158; parents and, 13, 43, 132,
    178; teachers and, 81, 132. *See also*
    Action-Reflection Learning Cycle;
    Unifying Five Words; Unifying
    seminars; unique potential
character culture, 195
Character First (Gauld), 50
cheating behavior, xviii
childhood experiences, 95, 212
childhood spirit, 213
Chinese proverbs, 114
Churchill, Sir Winston, 54, 97
"Clearing the Decks" in seminars, 125
cliff experience, 85–88
cocoon analogy, 174, 180–181, 194
Coleman Report, 174
community action program, 100
concern: about, 17; experiences of, 21;
    meetings to demonstrate, 211;
    parenting with, 190; as pathway to
    excellence, 168
confidentiality, 125

conscience: at center of learning, 81;
    definitions, 90–91; ego's
    relationship with, 92; parenting
    with, 189; in rigor-synergy-
    conscience process, 130, 142–146;
    as Unifying Principle, 26, 30–31
Consistency stage of learning process,
    102, 106
Coolidge, Calvin, 12
courage, 17, 20–21, 168, 178, 190
Cowardly Lion, 190
Coyle, Daniel, xix–xx, 45
critical thinking, 162–164
Culture Code (Coyle), xix–xx
culture of school. *See* Unifying culture
curiosity: about, 17; as ethic, 139;
    examples, 19–20; parenting with,
    190; purpose of, 178; risk-taking
    and, 96; as Unifying Word, 168

daimon, 3
Daly, Mary, 184
daydreams, 85–86
delayed gratification, 132–135
deliverables: challenges and mastery,
    206–209; family context, 212–214;
    meaningful relationships, 209–211;
    public speaking confidence,
    204–206; self-awareness, 199–204
Deming, W. Edwards, 51
destiny: academics and, 154–155;
    character and, 11–12, 157;
    importance of, 13, 15, 37; parents
    and, 175–177, 188; as Unifying
    Principle, 26, 28
developmental areas of IPSES, 99–101
difficult conversations, 210
discipline, 73, 206–208
Discovery Groups: about, xxii–xxiii,
    116–117; curriculum, 202–204;
    reflection process, 117

Eberhardt, Isabelle, 95
Edison, Thomas, 7

effort: performance/achievement compared to, 97, 152; as stage of learning process, 102, 106, 191
ego and conscience, 90–92, 143–145
Einstein, Albert, xxvii
Eisenhower, Dwight, 182–185
elevator analogy, 179
Emerson, Ralph Waldo, 4–6
emotion: character and, 121–122; negative emotional dispositions, 93–95; positive emotional dispositions, 94; self-regarding, 145; self-transcending, 145; in Unifying process, 89–90; unproductive feelings, 200
emotional development, xix, 100
emotional intelligence, 201–202
Emotional Intelligence (Goleman), 132–134
Emotional Intelligence 2.0 (Bradberry and Greaves), 202
English classwork, 155
equality, 148–150, 151
example, learning by, 18, 36
excellence: equality and, 151; exceptional families, 176; in Hyde's Unified School Community, 8; pathway to, 167–169; as stage of learning process, 103, 106, 191
expectations, 194

facilitators of seminars, 123
faith, 6–7
Family Days/Weekends, 213–214
Family Learning Center (FLC): about, 173–174; deepening parent relationship, 58–59; as deliverable, 213–214; family fundamentals for success, 174–178; Letting Go and Taking Hold process, 179–181, 214; personal struggles of parents, 192–193; principles, not personalities, raising children, 186–187, 194; priorities, 194–197; spiritual aspect of parenthood,

182–186. *See also* parents and families
farmers, 184
fear of heights, 85–88
Feather, William, 142
Feltti, Vincent, 95
Five Deeper Resources (IPSES), 99–101
Five Principles. *See* Unifying Five Principles
five qualities of teachers, 72–74
Five Words. *See* Unifying Five Words
FLC. *See* Family Learning Center (FLC)
foreign language classwork, 156
formal speaking, 206
Franklin, Benjamin, 91
Freud, Sigmund, 84, 90, 130
Frost, Robert, 56

Gandhi, Mahatma, 97
Gardner, Howard, xxvii
Gardner, John W., 14
Gauld, Laura, 194–195
Georgetown University study, xviii
Gibran, Kahlil, 28, 182
Goethe, Johann von, 13
Golden Rule, 14, 130
Goleman, Daniel, 132–134
Grant, Ken, 115–116
Greatest Generation, 55
Greaves, Jean, 202
growth, model of, 72
"head" in Unifying process, 82, 83, 86–88

head of school: as authority, 45, 186–187; ethics and, 47
"heart" in Unifying process, 82–83, 83, 86–88
Heraclitus, 11, 28, 167
hierarchy of Unifying process: about, 79–84; emotional cleansing and, 89–90; fear of heights example, 85–88; Five Deeper Resources

(IPSES), 99–101; head, 82, 83, 86–88; heart, 82–83, 83, 86–88; interfering experiences, 93–96; process of working through, 83–84; soul, 16–88, 83, 86–88; Unifying Five Lessons, 82, 96–98. *See also* Action-Reflection Learning Cycle; conscience; learning levels

higher power: humility and, 29; serenity prayer, 185–186; spiritual resources, 100; truth and, 32

high expectations, 73, 74–76

history classwork, 156

home as primary classroom, 18. *See also* parents and families

home school students, 149

homework for seminars, 123

humility: as ethic, 46–47; parenting with, 182, 189, 195; as Unifying Principle, 26, 29–30

Hurd, Paul, 74–76

imagination, 85–86

imitation process, 15–16, 138–139

inequality in education, 148–150

informal speaking, 206

inner search, 97. *See also* destiny

insightfulness, 160–162

inspiration, 195–197

integrity: about, 17; examples, 22–23; excellence and, 168; parenting with, 191; student's story of learning, 54

intellectual character, 100, 156–158

intellectual proficiency, 43–44, 100

intentional learning. *See* AICR academic practices

IPSES areas, 99–101

James, William, 55

Johnson, Samuel, 71

journals, 19–23, 155

Jung, Carl, 84

Kaufman, Scott, 84

kindergartners, xx, 45

King, Martin Luther, Jr., 98

Kleiser, Grenville, 16

"knowing thyself" focus, xxvii–xxviii

leadership: about, 17; examples, 21–22; opportunities, 208; parenting with, 191; unique potential and, 178. *See also* Brother's/Sister's Keepers

learning cycles. *See* Action-Reflection Learning Cycle

learning levels: conscience-centered, 81–82; student-centered, 81; subject-centered, 80; teacher-centered, 81

Letting Go and Taking Hold process, 179–181, 195, 214

life and cocoon analogy, 110–113

loyalty, 177

Malraux, Andre, 9

Mann, Horace, xxiv

marshmallow test, 132–134

mathematics classwork, 155

Mead, Margaret, 35

meaningful relationships, 209–211

Miller, Henry, 7

moral character, 156–158

Motions stage of learning process, 102, 106, 190–191

motivation of students, 150

Murray, W. H., 42–43

Myers-Briggs personality test, xxvi

National Assessment of Educational Progress (NAEP) tests, 148–149

National Institute of Mental Health, 50

NEDs (negative emotional dispositions), 93–95, 212–213

needs *vs.* wants, 187

negative emotional dispositions (NEDs), 93–95, 212–213

never lie-never quit ethic, 135–139

Newton, Isaac, 95
Nin, Anaïs, 118
Northrup, Christiane, 89

obstacles and opportunities, 195
Off-track stage of learning process,
101–102, 105–106, 179
"On Children" (Gibran), 182

parents and families: of alumni, 49; in
character development, 13, 48,
61–64; commitment of, 35,
104–106, 177; context as
deliverable, 212–214; family
wealth, xviii; home school students,
149; humility and, 30; schools
partnering with, 18–19, 25;
stepping up, 8–9; teaching to,
74–76; in traditional classrooms,
54–57, 58–59; Unifying culture
and, 41–43, 52; Unifying Five
Principles and, 35–38, 188–190;
Unifying Five Words and, 190–191;
unique potential concept and,
36–37. *See also* Family Learning
Center (FLC)
passivity of students, xxi
patience, 7
PEDs (positive emotional
dispositions), 94
performing arts program, 100
physical development, 100
positive emotional dispositions
(PEDs), 94
power struggles with children, 35
principals. *See* head of school
principles. *See* Unifying Five
Principles
priorities, 194–197
private conversations, 46
The Prophet (Gibran), 182
public speaking confidence, 204–206
purpose of life, 177. *See also* character;
destiny; unique potential

quitting response, 137, 143

rebels, xxi
reflection. *See* Action-Reflection
Learning Cycle
Reflections on Life (Carrel), 13
relationships, 209–211. *See also*
Brother's/Sister's Keepers; head of
school; parents and families;
teachers
respect, 8, 178
responsibility, 36, 164–167
rigor-synergy-conscience process:
conscience level, 130, 142–146;
curiosity ethic, 139, 143; delayed
gratification, 132–135, 143; equality
and, 129; never lie-never quit ethic,
135–139, 143; rigor level, 130,
131–140; synergy level, 130,
140–142, 144
risk-taking instincts, 96
"The Road Not Taken" (Frost), 56

scaffolding process, 81
school-family bonds. *See* parents and
families
school shootings, xviii
school-student relationship, 19
science classwork, 155
self-awareness, 199–204
self-discipline, 208
self-management, 202
self-regarding emotion, 145
self-transcending emotion, 145
serenity prayer, 185–186
Shakespeare, William, 4
sharing and synergy, 121–122
social awareness, 202
social development, 100
social growth, xix
social management, 202
"soul" in Unifying process, 16–88, 83,
86–88
Spencer, Herbert, 11
spirituality. *See* higher power

stages of learning: importance of readiness, 101–104; in-depth look at, 105–107

Stanford University's marshmallow test, 132–134

student-centered focus, 73

student-centered learning, 81

students: responsibilities in Unifying culture, 58–61; roles in traditional classrooms, 54–55; roles in Unifying culture, 51, 52–57 subconscious, 144–145. *See also* rigor-synergy-conscience process

subject-centered learning, 80

success and failure, valuing, 195

support for other's best, 98

synergy, 45–47, 121–122, 130, 140–142, 144

teachers: evaluations of, 60–61; parents partnering with, 66; qualities distinguishing, 72–74; responsibilities in Unifying culture, 68–76; roles in Unifying culture, 52, 66–68; students partnering with, xxiv–xxvii; teacher-centered learning, 81

test scores, emphasis on, 150. *See also* academics

TikTok app, xxiv

traditional education, xxiv–xxvii; character development, 50–51, 62; of culture, 49–50; growth and progress defined in, 79, 82, 103, 110; intellectual achievement emphasis, 69–70; parental role, 62; student responsibilities, 59; Unifying process compared to, 113–114

transformational challenges, 16, 178

trust, 46

truth: betting on, 97; honesty of teachers, 71–72; more important than harmony, 194; never lie-never quit ethic, 135–139, 143; parenting

with, 189; personal and professional honesty, 63; reverence for, 92; as Unifying Principle, 26, 31–32

twelve-step programs, 127

unconscious as central to intelligence, 85

Ungifted (Kaufman), 84

Unifying culture: accomplishments, xxiv; belief in unique gifts, 6; characteristics, 7–8; expectations of students, 59–61; synergy of, 45–47; traditional education comparison, 43–47, 49–51. *See also* head of school; parents and families; students; teachers; unique potential

Unifying Five Principles: commiting to, 25–26; goals of, 26–27; parents and, 35–38, 188–190. *See also* Brother's/Sister's Keepers; conscience; destiny; humility; truth

Unifying Five Words: about, 17; examples, 19–23; for excellence, 167–169; as "I" concepts, 26; parenting with, 190–191. *See also* concern; courage; curiosity; integrity; leadership

Unifying process: about, 96–98; commiting to, 104–106; focus of, xxiv–xxvii; goals and results, xxii–xxiv; importance of readiness to learn, 101–104; resources needed in, 177–178. *See also* Action-Reflection Learning Cycle; hierarchy of Unifying process

Unifying seminars: about, 119–120; guidelines, 126–127; structure of, 123–125; synergy of sharing in, 121–122

unique potential: academics and, 152–155; character and, 157; defining, 3–4; Emerson on, 4–6; faith required to fulfill, 6–7; goals and paths, 6; hierarchy of authority and, 180–181; parents and, 36–37,

175–177; patience and, 7; revolutionizing roles, 51–52; of teachers, 70–71; Unified School Community's belief in, 6. *See also* character; integrity

University of Chicago study on parents, 176

Wilde, Oscar, 97

youth culture, xii–xiii

ABOUT THE AUTHOR

Joseph W. Gauld, MA in mathematics, is the founder of Hyde Schools, reflecting his commitment to find a better way to prepare youth for life. This new process unified schools and families, leading him to write several books on parenting as well as on education. Hyde education has been featured in the media, including CBS's *60 Minutes*, NBC's *Today*, and ABC's *20/20*. Since the Hyde process unifies efforts beyond education, Gauld also has served as a consultant to other organizations. In 2016, Character.org chose him for its Lifetime Achievement in Character Education annual award.

www.ingramcontent.com/pod-product-compliance
Lightning Source LLC
Chambersburg PA
CBHW060313100426
42812CB00003B/772